22/7/74

Mum and Dad.

An "Un-Birthday" present!

From Mary.

ROSES

PETER COATS

 OCTOPUS BOOKS

Acknowledgments

The author and publishers wish to thank HM Queen Elizabeth II for her gracious permission to reproduce figure 61 from the Royal Collection.

The author also wishes to express his grateful thanks to the following people, who have given him advice and encouragement: Le Vicomte de Noailles; Mrs Day, Organising Secretary of Queen Alexandra's Nursing Fund; H. Edland Esq. of the National Rose Society; Simon Fleet Esq.; Mrs Langley Moore; Miss Nancy Lindsay; J. Russell Esq. of the Sunningdale Nurseries; Miss Julia Clements; Kenneth Snowman Esq.; T. Stageman Esq. of the Royal Horticultural Society Library, London, and Dr Stearn of the Natural History Museum. Hugh Robson Esq. did the drawings for figures 2, 3, 9, 10, 27, 30, 84, 97, 98, 108, 110, 111, 113, 114, and pages 21, 29, 47, and 65.

The author and publishers also wish to thank the following owners and collectors, who have made available objects from their collections: The Lady Juliet Duff, figure 57; Cecil Beaton Esq., figures 26, 88, 117; Charles Gregory Esq.; C. V. Jacobs Esq., figure 58; Oliver Messel Esq., figure 68; H. Wheatcroft Esq.; Laurence Whistler Esq., figure 119. J. E. Downward, figure 89. Figure 5 is reproduced by kind permission of the Royal Institute of British Architects; figures 14, 20 by courtesy of the National Portrait Gallery, London; figure 24 by courtesy of the National Gallery of Scotland; figure 72 by courtesy of the Trustees, National Gallery, London, and © by SPADEM, Paris 1962. Figures 7, 8, 34, 36, 40 appear by courtesy of the British Museum; figures 13, 39, 47, 56, 63, 64, 69, 74, 75, 77 by courtesy of the Victoria and Albert Museum; figure 71 by courtesy of the New York Public Library; and figure 59, the Musée de Strasbourg.

Figures 1, 12, 17, 19, 25, 37, 52, 53, 85, 86 are reproduced by permission of the Royal Horticultural Society Library; figures 35, 60, 65, by permission of the Witt Library, Courtauld Institute of Art; figures 44, 73, 83, 118 by permission of the Musée des Arts Décoratifs; figure 72 by permission of the Arts Council of Great Britain.

Figure 41 is reproduced by courtesy of the National Film Archive; figure 78 by courtesy of Messrs Tiffany, New York; figure 76 by courtesy of Messrs Spinks, London; figure 51 by courtesy of *Punch*.

Figures 6, 11, 21, 22, 45 were provided by the Mansell Collection; figures 14, 20 by the National Portrait Gallery; figures 7, 8, 36, 40 by the British Museum; figure 13 by the Victoria and Albert Museum; figure 59, by the Archives Photographiques, Paris.

Figure 28 is by the Radio Times Hulton Picture Library; figure 67 by Alinari (18991); figure 70 by EMI Ltd, London; figure 46 by Anderson (11060); figure 24 is by Messrs Annans, Glasgow; figures 44, 83, 118 are by Helène Adant, Paris; figure 72 by R. B. Fleming and Co. Ltd.; figure 62 by Sperryns Ltd.; figure 61 by E. E. Swain Ltd., Hunstanton; and figure 119 by Derek Sprange Ltd.

Figures 18, 94, 95, 96, 97, 115, 116 were photographed by the author. All other photographs were taken for this book by John Hedgcoe.

This edition first published 1973 by
OCTOPUS BOOKS LIMITED
59 Grosvenor Street, London W 1

ISBN 0 7064 0055 0

© 1962 by Peter Coats

Produced by Mandarin Publishers Limited
77a Marble Road, North Point, Hong Kong
and printed in Hong Kong

Preceding page:
Zambra, a brilliant floribunda rose with double flowers, raised by the celebrated firm of Meilland.

Contents

Rosa Indica   *Rosier du Bengale Cent feuilles*

4

THE ROSE IN HISTORY

2 In the *Georgics* Virgil praises the roses of Paestum which flowered, twice a year, *'biferique rosaria Paesti'*.

1 *(opposite)* Pierre Joseph Redouté (1759–1840), most celebrated of all painters of roses, drew this *Rosa Indica*, rose of Bengal, which first flowered in England in 1810.

June of the iris and the rose.
The rose not English as we fondly think.
Anacreon and Bion sang the rose;
And Rhodes the isle whose very name means rose
Struck roses on her coins;
Pliny made lists and Roman libertines
Made wreaths to wear among the flutes and wines;
The young Crusaders found the Syrian rose
Springing from Saracenic quoins,
And China opened her shut gate
To let her roses through, and Persian shrines
Of poetry and painting gave the rose.

V. Sackville-West

NO FLOWER HAS BEEN SO EXTOLLED in writing as the rose, or has so long a history of admiration. Shakespeare mentions roses more than sixty times; the Bible, however, only twice. For the rose with which the desert was to blossom was apparently not a rose at all but an asphodel, while the Rose of Sharon is the name we give now to that most workaday of garden plants, St John's Wort.

Roses crowned the heads of Roman revellers and there are many references to them among Roman writers. An anonymous Latin poet wrote:

'The rose is the flower of Venus: in order that her sweet thefts might be concealed, Love dedicated to Harpocrates, the god of silence, this gift of his mother. Hence the host hangs over his friendly table a rose, that the guests underneath it may know how to keep silence as to what is said'. This is the origin of the phrase, *sub rosa*.

Roses also played a great part in the public games so beloved by the Romans, at which the boxes of the spectators were looped and festooned with thousands of flowers, and the winners were garlanded with them. Martial constantly mentions roses as decorations of Roman banquets, and the extravagant and frivolous Emperor, Elagabalus, who made a dancer his Commander-in-Chief, and a hairdresser his Minister of Supply, is said to have caused the death of several of his guests at a feast by showering them with rose petals so that they were completely buried and suffocated.

3 Roses played a decorative part in Roman festivals: here they wreath a standard.

4 Henry II and his mistress Rosamond, who is said to have been poisoned by his jealous Queen. The striped rose Rosa Mundi is believed to have been named after her.

It was no metaphor to the Romans but an allusion to a literal fact, when they talked of sleeping upon beds of roses. Cicero in his third oration against Verres, when charging the proconsul with luxurious habits, stated that he had made the tour of Sicily seated upon roses. Seneca even says that a Sybarite of the name of Smyrndiride was unable to sleep if one of the rose petals on his bed happened to be curled. At a feast which Cleopatra gave to Mark Antony the floor of the hall was covered with fresh roses to the depth of eighteen inches. At a fête given by Nero at Baiae the sum of four millions of sesterces or about twenty thousand pounds was incurred for roses.

Throughout the history of Imperial Rome roses were not only used as a decoration at feasts, but festivals of roses were common events, though they never became fixed public festivals. Frequent occasions of this kind were the *Dies Rosationis* which were commemorative services for the dead, when bereaved families would meet at a grave and deck it with roses.

With the coming of Christianity all this changed, and roses, which had a bad reputation because of their associations with pagan revels and Roman excess, played little part in the early ceremonies of the church. But, inevitably, the rose was reinstated: its petals were held to represent Christ's five wounds; red roses were taken as the symbol of the blood of the early Martyrs, for the rose, in its beauty and mystic significance, was indispensable.

It was soon to be embodied in ecclesiastical architecture itself. Early in the Middle Ages, church and cathedral windows came to be made in the form of roses; it is said that the idea of these rose-windows, as they came to be called, circular and highly decorative, that are often found in Transitional and early Gothic cathedrals, was brought to France by returning Crusaders. It is certainly true that the Mosque of Ibn Touloun in Cairo has windows in the form of cusped circles which are much like the rose-windows we know. By the end of the twelfth century, rose-windows had become usual features of ecclesiastical buildings in France, and, to a lesser degree, in England. The rose-windows at Laon and Chartres in France are particularly beautiful, while in England there are fine examples at York, Westminster and Lincoln, where there is a famous rose-window known as 'the Dean's Eye'. Rose-windows were not all; in the Chapter House in York Minster there is an inscription which reads *Ut rosa flos florum sic est domus domorum*, 'as the rose is the flower of flowers this is the house of all houses'.

At the ancient Abbey of Hildesheim in Germany, there are several legends connected with the thousand-year-old rose tree which grows against its walls. One says that the rose was planted by Charlemagne himself, but another, more attractive, legend, quotes the story of the Emperor Ludwig. The Emperor, it appears, lost his way while hunting wild boar in the thick forest which at that period surrounded the area of Hildesheim. Dusk fell, and he had to spend the night in the open. All around roamed wild beasts, so he improvised an altar by hanging his chain and golden crucifix onto a thorn-bush and prayed for protection during the long, dark night. He woke safely, and in the morning his retinue found him, and discovered that the bush had been transformed overnight into a rose tree. The Emperor ordered that a chapel should be built on the site, and it is said that this chapel is the forerunner of the great cathedral that we see today. The rose tree is thirty feet high and covers forty feet of wall, and is recorded to have flowered for over a thousand years. The Abbey itself was damaged by air-raids during the Second World War but in spite of all, the rose tree lives on.

In England a rose legend which dates from the early Middle Ages is that of Fair Rosamond, mistress of Henry II; she was the daughter of Walter de Clifford, and her story has been the basis of many legends and ballads. Stow, the sixteenth-century chronicler and antiquary, relates of her, 'Rosamond, the fayre daughter of Walter Lord Clifford, concubine to King Henry II (poisoned by Queen Eleanor, as some thought), died at Woodstocke, where King Henry had made for her a house of wonderful working so that no man or woman could come to her but that was instructed by the King: the house...was named Labyrinthus...wrought like unto a knot in a garden, called a maze; but it was commonly said that lastly the Queene came to her by a clue of thriddle or silk, and so dealt with her that she lived not long after; but when she was dead she was buried at Godstone in a house of nunnes, beside Oxford, with these verses on her tombe:

> Hic jacet in tumba Rosa Mundi, non Rosa Munda.
> Non redolet, sed olet, quae redolere solet.'

The verses are not very complimentary and might be translated,

> Here rose the graced, not rose the chaste, reposes;
> The scent that rises is no scent of roses.

Samuel Daniel, the 'New Shepherd Late Up Sprong' of Spenser's *Colin Clout*, wrote poor Rosamond's tale in *The Complaynte of Rosamond*, 1592, a poem in rhyme royal; and Addison wrote an opera about her. The beautiful rose, Rosa Mundi, finest and gayest of all the striped roses in our gardens today, is said to be named after Rosamond.

It seems curious that one of the most brutal of civil wars in England should bear the romantic name of the Wars of the Roses which racked England during the reigns of Henry VI, Edward IV

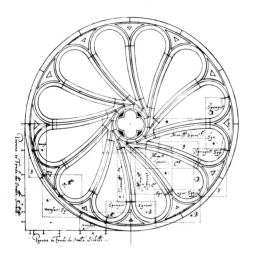

5 An architectural design for a rose-window, made in England in 1599.

6 The famous rose-window over the south transept of York Cathedral, dating from the thirteenth century.

and Richard III. They were marked by a brutality unknown in the history of England before or since. The wars began with the demand of the Yorkist Lords for the dismissal of the Lancastrian element in the weak and vacillating council of King Henry VI. Shakespeare sets the scene in the Temple Garden where a violent quarrel breaks out between the ambitious Richard Plantagenet and the energetic Earl of Warwick (the Kingmaker), who pick white roses and wear them as their symbol, and on the other side, the Earl of Somerset and the Earl of Suffolk who choose red.

7, 8 Two illustrations from the fourteenth-century manuscript, *Romaunt de la Rose*, the earliest of all English poems about a rose. It is a translation, partly by Chaucer, of an earlier French poem.

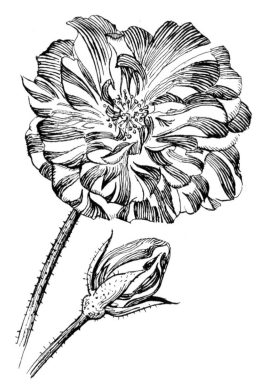

9 Rosa Mundi, of the *Gallica* group, has petals striped in carmine and white.

10 The thousand-year-old rose tree which grows against the walls of Hildesheim Cathedral in Germany has legendary connections with Charlemagne and the Emperor Ludwig.

PLANTAGENET: Since you are tongue-tied and so loath to speak,
In dumb significants proclaim your thoughts:
Let him that is a true-born gentleman
And stands upon the honour of his birth,
If he suppose that I have pleaded truth,
From off this briar pluck a white rose with me.

SOMERSET: Let him that is no coward nor no flatterer,
But dare maintain the party of the truth,
Pluck a red rose from off this thorn with me.

WARWICK: I love no colours, and, without all colour
Of base insinuating flattery
I pluck this white rose with Plantagenet.

SUFFOLK: I pluck this red rose with young Somerset
And say withal I think he held the right.

VERNON: Stay, lords and gentlemen, and pluck no more,
Till you conclude that he upon whose side
The fewest roses are cropp'd from the tree,
Shall yield the other in the right opinion.

However the conflict may have begun, throughout the thirty blood-soaked years of the Wars of the Roses, it is certain that the Red Rose of Lancaster and the White Rose of York were the symbols of the warring factions, though these badges by no means superseded the private devices of the various great lords, such as the Falcon and Fetterlock of the Duke of York, the *Rose en Soleil* of Edward IV, and the Crowned Swan of Margaret of Anjou. With the defeat and death of the Yorkist Richard III, however, the Lancastrian cause triumphed. Peace returned and was soon consolidated by the politic marriage of Henry Tudor, the new King Henry VII, to the Plantagenet princess Elizabeth of York; the flower which was then adopted as the Royal device, and which henceforward appeared everywhere, carved, cast, embroidered and printed (for in 1477 Caxton had introduced printing into England), was the Red and White Tudor rose.

Since the Middle Ages, roses have always played an important part in heraldry, and in the language of heraldry there are four different rose devices. The most usual is the rose with five petals and a bold boss of stamens, with the five sepals' points showing between the petals; if the sepals are emblazoned in a different colour to the petals, the rose is referred to as 'barbed', and if the boss is different, the rose is described as 'seeded'. The Tudor Rose is double, with white and red petals for the houses of York and Lancaster. The *Rose en Soleil*, cognizance of Edward IV, is a rose with a sun's rays spreading beyond the petals. Last, there is the 'slipped' rose which, when surmounted by the Royal Crown, is the Badge of England [figure 18].

Many Kings and Queens of England have had roses on their

devices. Before Edward IV's *Rose en Soleil*, there was the gold rose 'stalked proper' of Edward I. Henry IV's was a red rose; Elizabeth's a Tudor rose with the legend 'A rose without a thorn'. Queen Anne, in whose reign England and Scotland were united, had for emblem a rose and thistle growing from one stem: this figures on the King's Colour of the 2nd Battalion Scots Guards.

The rose is the adopted flower of several American States.

The District of Columbia unofficially claims the American Beauty rose, and Georgia, the White Cherokee rose. The rose is the flower of New York State, the wild rose that of Iowa, and the prairie rose that of North Dakota.

11 The Wars of the Roses (1455–85) were named after the quarrel between the Dukes of York and Lancaster in the garden of the Temple in London, where each plucked a rose of a different colour.

The rose is always connected with the Jacobites, but how the single white rose became their emblem is uncertain; was it because the Old Pretender's father had once been Duke of York (the 'Jacobite' rose is the same as the York rose), or was it because roses were blooming in Scotland when the Duke of Mar landed there in 1715, and again when Prince Charles raised his standard

11

12 An illustration by Alfred Parsons in Ellen Wilmott's *Genus Rosa*, published in 1914. These rose-hips show his feeling for the colour and character of growing things.

in 1745, and adherents of the Jacobite cause welcomed the invaders with roses? Or was it because, in the first short-lived enthusiasm, the rush of recruits to the royal headquarters was such that the Jacobites ran out of white cockades, which were certainly their emblem too, and used white roses instead? But tradition will always link white roses with the Stuarts, and Bonnie Prince Charlie is said to have worn one in his bonnet as he marched triumphantly to Derby.

Fourteen years after the failure of the '45 rising, in 1759, the *Annus Mirabilis* when victory after victory wreathed the British arms with laurels, the Battle of Minden was fought against the French, and six British regiments won fame; and one in particular, the Lancashire Fusiliers. So heavy were their losses on that day that Prince Ferdinand of Brunswick, commanding the Allied Army, directed that the regiment should be excused from further

13 Nicholas Hilliard
(1537–1619), one of the
first English miniature
painters, excelled at
romantic portraits such
as this, an anonymous
Elizabethan gallant in
a rose garden.

13

14 *(right)* Henry VII of England (1457–1509) holding the rose that symbolized the fusion of the York and Lancaster factions, by an unknown artist. *(above)* The rose also figured prominently in his coinage.

duty. This indulgence the Commanding Officer, Colonel Kingsley, refused to accept, and a general order, dated August 1759, records that 'Kingsley's regiment, at its own request, will resume its position of duty in the line'. Tradition relates that, before the battle, the regiment was posted in a rose garden, with flowers from which the men decked their hats during the fray. Ever since, the glorious memories of the day have been recalled by the regimental custom of wearing Minden roses in their caps on August 1. They are still nicknamed the 'Minden Boys'.

Curiously enough, the rose is not part of the crest of the Lancashire Fusiliers, though roses figure prominently in the crests of many other regiments, specially Yorkshire ones. The East Lancashire Regiment's crest is a sphinx and a rose, with the

15 A ship bearing a single rose denotes the birth of English sea-power; on the reverse is stamped a rose design which gave the name to the Rose Noble, a coin of Edward IV in 1465.

16 This memorial emblem was printed and secretly circulated after the 1745 Jacobite Rebellion. It bears the names of some who suffered for the Jacobite cause.

motto *Spectamur Agendo* (let us be judged by our actions) while the Loyal Regiment has the Rose of Lancaster on the crest with the motto *Loyauté m'oblige*. The Yorkshire Hussars has, as crest, a rose crowned.

The glorious British victory of Minden caused consternation at Versailles; a few weeks after the battle Madame de Pompadour in a letter to the wife of Marshal Contades wrote, 'This horrible defeat at Minden is the most melancholy check we have received during the whole war. I am sorry for both your sake and mine, that it should have been Monsieur Contades who was there.'

Madame de Pompadour was often painted holding a rose, and one rose, at least, has come down to us, *La Belle de Crécy*, which is said to have been one of her favourites. Of it, and two other delightful old roses, Sacheverell Sitwell has said, 'Belle de Crécy is a rose found growing in the garden of Madame de Pompadour. The scent of it takes you in a breath into the eighteenth century, while the rose pink petals and jade green leaves make one think of the bows and ribbons of the Pompadour by Boucher... Another old rose, Madame de Roche Lambert, of the time of Louis Philippe, has a leaf growing like a cockade out of the side of the flower, and it is the most coquettishly prim rose imaginable. Could one meet the Abbess of a convent for noble nuns driving in her carriage, this rose, with its cockade, should be decorating her coachman's hat. Madame Gardy, a white rose with a flat flower, as though halved with a knife, is one more of the early nineteenth-century roses which have all the fragrance of the past.'

Madame de Pompadour gave her name to a particular shade of rose, but more famous and still well known today is the colour Rose du Barry, called after Madame de Pompadour's successor in the affection of Louis XV. The beautiful and kindly Madame du Barry loved roses too, and her bedroom at Versailles, a triumph of the interior decorator's art, was lavishly decorated with them. The bed, of elaborately carved wood, was gilded by the celebrated Clagny. Its four slender pillars held aloft a canopy of roses, from which hung silk curtains embroidered by a design of tumbling showers of the same flower. Similar rich material was used for the window curtains and for the many small chairs grouped, as in a theatre, before the steps which led up to the favourite's bed; it was on these chairs that Madame du Barry's little Court would sit, and watch the elaborate performance of her *levée*, when Madame du Barry would drink her coffee, read her correspondence, and decide which dress she would wear that day. For an ordinary occasion it might be a simple dress made of Indian Muslin sent to her by Tippoo Sahib; for a great function, a dress of splendour such as the one she wore for the marriage of the Comte d'Artois '...*chiné en argent, brodé en papillons verts et roses; les pompons, la palatine et la tour de cou brodé de petites*

15

18 Roses played an important part in mediaeval heraldry: this 'slipped' rose is the badge of England.

19 *(right)* Alfred Parsons' version of *Rosa indica semperflorens.*

17 *(opposite) Rosa foetida bicolor* by Alfred Parsons. This Austrian copper briar is the parent of most of the orange and two-toned hybrids of today.

'roses'. This dress is said to have cost over three thousand pounds. Poor Madame du Barry; long after Louis was dead, and after twenty years of living quietly, far from Versailles, the Revolution overtook her and she was denounced as Mistress of a King of France, imprisoned and guillotined.

We do not know, though it is quite possible, whether Madame du Barry made the acquaintance of another woman while both were imprisoned. The latter, more fortunate than Madame du Barry, escaped death in the Revolution, and thereafter lived a remarkable life. Her name will ever be connected with roses – Joséphine de Beauharnais.

In June 1763, in the month of roses, she was born in Martinique, and christened Rose. Her destiny was to be one of the strangest and most splendid imaginable, and her character, slight and elusive, as might be expected of *un oiseau des îles,* distils its own faint, but clinging perfume, as we turn the pages of her husband's thunderous career. Joséphine Rose was betrothed when only sixteen to the Vicomte de Beauharnais and shipped unceremoniously to France by her family, who had two other daughters to marry off. Widowed in the Revolution, her fortunes were at a low ebb, when suddenly, like a thunderclap, a thin, badly-dressed young general, Napoleon Bonaparte, came into her life. Joséphine's influential friends foretold a great future for him, and when he fell passionately in love with her, and proposed marriage, they urged her to accept him. She did, for to her marriage spelt security, though not love, and she never, until it was too late, appreciated the depth of Napoleon's feeling for

20   Queen Elizabeth I, whose badge was the red and white Tudor rose, wears a rose in her ruff. Dated 1593, it is by an unknown artist.

21   The Château of Malmaison, where the Empress Joséphine assembled her collection of roses.

22   *(opposite)* François Drouais (1727–75) painted this portrait of Madame du Barry as Flora.

23 One of the most famous of rose growers, the Empress Joséphine, wife of Napoleon I.

24 A detail of Boucher's portrait of Madame de Pompadour, in the National Gallery of Scotland.

her. The security and splendour of her marriage enabled her, for the first time, to gratify her passion, long-dormant perhaps, for plants and gardening.

In 1798 she acquired Malmaison, the place whose name is forever linked with hers, and there she created gardens which became the sensation of Europe. These were not gardens of the *ancien régime* like those at Versailles, but gardens almost like our own today, though on a larger scale. Joséphine really loved plants and knew about them. She did not care only for terraces and fountains, but loved flowers, spending fortunes on financing expeditions to the East and to South Africa to collect new specimens (she had an odd penchant for *Ericas*). She grew the first dahlias in France, and in that courtlier age, although throughout her career as Bonaparte's wife France was at war with England, plants destined for Joséphine, but intercepted by British ships on the high seas, were allowed to pass through the blockade by order of the Prince Regent himself. Furthermore throughout the war with England, the head gardener at Malmaison was a Scot, Monsieur Hewartson. Above all, Joséphine loved roses and would spend hours in her garden tending them. Many of the roses she grew are still with us today. To perpetuate their beauty, Joséphine commanded Redouté, among the greatest of flower potraitists, to paint their likenesses; these were collected and published in what must surely be one of the most sumptuous of all flower books, *Les Roses*. Those were happy days at Malmaison, when the Empire was young, and the Emperor would relax and play Blind Man's Buff with his step-daughter Hortense under the trees, while Joséphine picked roses and planned new borders, and planted cedars to commemorate victories; but they did not last long, barely fifteen years. Divorced wife of a fallen Emperor, Joséphine passed her last sad days at Malmaison and died in 1814.

The gardens at Malmaison fell into neglect and today, though the château is there for us to see, there is little of the garden that recalls its old glory, only the cedar of Marengo still casts its shadow on the lawn. Yet overall still broods the gentle spirit of Joséphine. In the tragic days of June 1815 between Waterloo and St Helena, Napoleon passed a few days at Malmaison as the guest of Hortense. There is great pathos in his words which she records: 'One evening, the Emperor said to me "How charming it is at Malmaison, what a pity it is, Hortense, that we cannot stay here". And again "How the spirit of Joséphine pervades this place. How graceful she was... I can almost see her walking in the garden among the flowers".' June 1815 – a month of roses, too. Two years later Redouté's great volume *Les Roses* was published, not, as it should have been, dedicated to the Empress, but to a member of the newly restored Royal Family – for politics play their part in horticulture too.

25 Redouté's picture of *Rosa myriacantha*, one
of the Burnet roses or Scotch briars, which has
strongly scented flowers, twigs covered with
prickles and shining black hips.

26 Hybrid Tea rose Caroline Testout, pink and sweetly scented. First introduced in 1890, here photographed by Cecil Beaton.

Queen Alexandra's Rose Day was the first of all flag days, and the first time it was held, on June 26, 1912, more than twenty thousand pounds was collected in the streets of London. Since then the total has risen to over fifty thousand pounds for London alone, and as much again for the rest of England: and since 1912 the idea of flag days has spread all over the world. How then did the idea, which was entirely Queen Alexandra's own, originally start? Alexandra was a Danish princess and came from the land of Hans Andersen, a land of fairy stories. In a village outside Copenhagen there lived a poor priest who never had enough money to help all the sick and crippled children who came to him for aid; and he could not think of any way of raising money until the idea came to him to sell the sweet-smelling roses which grew in the hedgerow round his garden, that he dearly loved, and which he thought of as his only luxury. So he sold his roses, and with the money he was able to help his children. This went on for many years, and the story of the old priest who deprived himself of his beloved roses to help the poor reached the ears of a beautiful princess, afterwards Queen Alexandra, who one day visited him in his little house. She never forgot the old priest and his roses, and many years later she commissioned Miss Christine May Beeman, the famous charity worker, to organize the first Rose Day, and with a typically imaginative touch suggested that

27 In 1759 British troops wearing roses in their caps won a great victory at the Battle of Minden.

28 The first Alexandra Rose Day was held on June 26, 1912: the widowed Queen Alexandra and her daughter Princess Victoria driving through Trafalgar Square, London.

the roses should not be counterparts of the highly cultivated garden varieties of roses then so fashionable, but simple wild roses, like those of the priest.

The first Rose Day took London by storm: fifteen hundred women, in the tight skirts and cart-wheel hats of 1912, 'held up' the people of London in the good cause of charity, and the climax of the day was the drive of the Rose-Queen, Alexandra, by then an old, but still beautiful lady, in a rose-decked carriage through the streets of London [figure 28].

MEDICINE AND COOKERY

29 John Parkinson, who listed a number of domestic uses for the rose in his great garden classic *Paradisus*, published in 1629.

IN THE REIGN OF ELIZABETH I, in 1597, one of the first great English books of flowers and plants was published, Gerard's *Herball*. In it, in one impressive paragraph, the rose is extolled:

'The plant of Roses, though it be a shrub full of prickles, yet it has beene more fit and convenient to have placed it with the most glorious flowers of the worlde, than to insert the same here among base and thornie shrubs: for the Rose doth deserve the chiefest and most principall place among all flowers whatsoever, being not only esteemed for his beautie, vertues, and his flagrant *(sic)* and odiferous smell; but also because it is the honour and ornament of our English Scepter, as by the conjunction apeereth in the uniting of these two most royall houses of Lancaster and Yorke.'

Elsewhere, Gerard writes lines which are oddly apposite in this space age: 'Who would look up dangerously at planets that might look safely down at plants'?

In the following century, in 1629, another great garden classic appeared, Parkinson's *Paradisus,* illustrated with woodcuts. Like Gerard, Parkinson is full of praise for the rose and sets down its qualities and divers uses thus:

'The Rose is of exceeding great use with us; for the Damaske Rose (besides the super-excellent sweete water it yeeldeth being distilled, or the perfume of the leaves being dryed, serving to fill sweet bags) serveth to cause solubleness of the body, made into a Syrupe, or preserved with Sugar moist or dry candid... The white Rose is much used for the cooling of heate in the eyes; divers doe make an excellent yellow colour of the juyce of white Roses, wherein some Allome is dissolved, to colour flowers or pictures.'

Culpeper (1616) states that roses are governed by Jupiter, Venus and the moon, and suggests that every part of the rose – the petals, leaves and hips, etc – can be used in many forms as medicine. 'A decoction of red roses made with wine is very good for the headache, pain in the eyes, throat and gums – while the husks of the roses with the beards and nails are binding and cooling...' For a dry conserve he recommends Sugar of roses as a cordial to strengthen the heart and raise the spirits; 'while a syrup of Damask roses, made with agaric, is forcible in working on melancholic humours, itch, tetters and the French Disease'. We see that not only was the rose used medicinally, but all its

30 The Indian Princess Nur Mahal and her husband the Great Mogul: she first discovered how to make attar of roses.

parts were in demand in the confection of sweetmeats and perfumes. From a famous book of simples, *A Queen's Delight* (1695), comes this recipe for candied rose petals, which in modern English runs:

'Dip small rose petals in beaten egg-white or weak gum Arabic and lay on a greaseproof paper sheet covered with caster sugar. Then sprinkle the petals both sides with sugar, leaving them to dry in a warm place, or cool oven. These can be stored in a jar with sheets of paper in between layers, and used for decoration on cakes or as sweetmeats. A few spots of cochineal added to the egg will help the colouring.'

And from another, charmingly named, old book, *The Queen's Closet Opened,* compiled by Queen Henrietta Maria's cook, comes a recipe for 'The King's Perfume':

'Take twelve spoonfuls of bright red rose-water, the weight of sixpence of powder of sugar, and boyl it on hot embers and coals softly, and the house will smell as though it were full of roses, but you must burn the sweet Cypress wood before to take away the gross ayre'.

In our own times in Calabria, the poorest part of Italy, the peasants make a liqueur of roses which is strongly scented, and which is said to have not only an inebriating, but also an aphrodisiac effect, *Sangue di Rose,* Rose's Blood. It is made of the rose flowers themselves, not the hips. Even in World War II rose-hips were used as a substitute for Vitamin C.

25

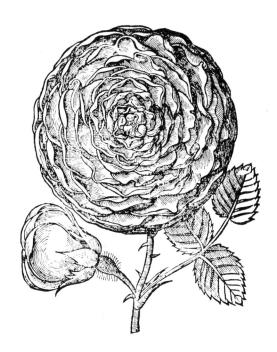

32 *Rosa hollandica*, a woodcut from Gerard's *Herball* published in 1597.

31 A sixteenth-century housewife listens to a discourse on the virtues and properties of the rose: from Champier's *Rosa gallica*, published in Paris in 1515.

Attar of roses – the essential oil of the rose from which all rose perfumes are made – has been highly valued through the centuries, especially in the East. Eighteenth-century travellers to India described acres of rose trees at Ghazeepore, which were cultivated for distillation, and making attar: and claimed that it was Princess Nur Mahal who discovered how attar could most easily be extracted, after having caused a large tank to be filled with roses when she and the Great Mogul were to be rowed on it. Finding that the sun's heat caused the rose oil to film the surface of the water, Nur Mahal commanded that the oil should be taken up with fine cotton wool, put into bottles and carefully sealed.

Beautiful as well as practical, Nur Mahal had a stormy, though on the whole successful, life. Soon after she first found favour with the Emperor, his five favourite wives died mysteriously, in quick succession, and soon Nur Mahal was all-powerful and intalled as Empress. She married her niece Mumtaz Mahal to the heir to the throne. (It was for Mumtaz Mahal that her husband, Shah Jehan, built the most beautiful tomb the world has ever seen, the Taj Mahal.) Doubtless, Nur Mahal passed on to her niece much useful advice – attar-making amongst it – but it is not known whether in India at that date, 1650, pot-pourri was ever used.

Pot-pourri, even in these busy times, is well worth making, as a bowl of it will give a delicious hint of incense to any room. No real need to use the endless (and difficult to find) ingredients recommended by the Victorians. There is a simple and comparatively quick way of making pot-pourri, if you follow these instructions:

33 *Springtime*, an engraving by P. van der Heyde, illustrating a scene of garden activity in 1570.

Cut your roses when the dew has dried and the warm sun has brought out their scent, but not yet begun to fade them. Separate the petals from the centres, bruising them as little as possible, and sprinkle them lightly with some salt; dry them thoroughly by spreading them on paper in an airy room, or, if there is no wind, on a sheet in the open air.

Make a well balanced blend by using light-scented tea rose petals with some of fuller-bodied scent. If you like, add small handfuls of other dried flowers and leaves, such as heliotrope, mignonette, jasmine, pinks, Parma violets, some dried scented geranium leaves, lemon verbena, rosemary or bay. Take $\frac{1}{2}$ oz. each of cloves, mace, cinnamon, allspice, crushed coriander and cardamom seeds (all of which can be found at most grocers) and 1 oz. each of gum storax and gum benzoin. Salt lightly.

Add other fragrances to the rose petal mixture. You can use all or only some of the ingredients suggested here, but the rose scent should dominate the whole. Add spices, a pinch at a time, sniffing it constantly. When the ingredients are thoroughly blended, sprinkle with a little alcohol or brandy. Then place the pot-pourri in a glass jar and keep it tightly stoppered for four or five weeks, stirring it occasionally. When needed, set it out in open bowls.

27

THE ROSE
IN LITERATURE

IN POETRY THE ROSE'S QUALITY and characteristics lend themselves enchantingly to metaphor and comparison: a rose's beauty first and foremost; its short life; its sweetness; its colour, scarlet or pink (yellow roses play little part in poetry) to which it is so easy to liken the beloved's mouth and cheeks. Leigh Hunt cried

> And what a red mouth has the rose,
> The woman of the flowers.

So it is the world over. In Malaya the very word for Rose and Woman is synonymous, and poets everywhere have composed their own variations on these accepted themes.

A very early poem in which the Rose played an important part, being endowed with human qualities or at least human attractions, for a rose bud is the heroine of the tale, is the *Romaunt de la Rose*. This epic poem, more than 7,000 lines of it, is a translation, in part by Chaucer, from the earlier French *Roman de la Rose,* which was written in the mid-thirteenth century. The story is the old one of the search for the unattainable, and describes a lover's dream, during which the hero passes the Garden of Mirth and is tempted to enter by an allegorical character, Idleness. Within the garden he meets several other characters, some pleasant, others less so, the God of Love, Gladness, Bialacoil (Bel Acceuil, Welcome), False Semblant, Danger, Wikkid Tungue and others. He falls in love with a rose bud he sees reflected in the Fountain of Narcissus, and in spite of his misgivings he tries to approach the flower:

> But anguished and full of thought
> I felt more woe than wounds ere wrought
> And yet I felt I had to go
> Towards the Rose that pleased me so.

The lover is helped or hindered by the various personalities of the garden, and at last success appears probable:

> Towards the Rose tree fast I drew
> But thorns much sharper then than now
> Were there – and thistles thick
> And brambles, too, to scratch and prick.

34 *(opposite)* A fifteenth-century Persian prince in a rose-patterned dress poses, rose in hand.

29

But then he has qualms that the owner of the garden may have something to say:

> Lest with anger would be fraught
> The Lord who had the garden wrought?

Finally, having become the bondsman of the God of Love, he takes useful hints from him (like tipping the maid) as to how to succeed in his suit, only to find that Jealousy has enclosed the rose in an impenetrable rampart. The poem is not only romantic but satirical, poking fun at the society of the time, the Church and women's ways generally. It was often illustrated in ancient manuscripts, of which some of the finest are in the British Museum.

Shakespeare uses the rose in more than sixty similes, almost always to symbolize perfection.

> The expectancy and rose of the fair state,
> The glass of fashion and the mould of form,
> The observed of all observers . . .

35 *L'Inspiration Favorable*, an engraving from the picture by Fragonard.

36 A garden in the Middle Ages, an illustration
to Chaucer's *Romaunt de la Rose*, fifteenth
century.

is how he describes the pre-eminence of the youthful Hamlet;
and in *Love's Labour's Lost*, Berowne uses the image of the
flower to typify summer and its delights:

> At Christmas I no more desire a rose
> Than wish a snow in May's new fangled mirth,
> But like of each thing that in season grows.

About the romantic, luckless Richard II he writes,

31

Στέφου δη με και λύρα εα
Παρα τοις Διονυσα σικοις.
Μετα Κόρης βαθυκολπω
Ρυθμοισι εφαντικοις
Πεπυκασμενος Χορευσω

Anacreon Ode V.

38 The crest of Henry Wise, gardener to Queen Anne: 'a demy-lion argent holding a damask rose, stalked, and seeded proper'.

39 A Turkish-Cypriot plate dating from the early fifteenth century, bearing a stylized design of roses and tulips.

37 *(opposite)* The frontispiece to Redouté's major work *Les Roses*, published in Paris in 1817. The Greek quotation is from Anacreon's *Fifth Ode*; 'Crown me and in your sacred grove I'll sing, and with full-breasted Cora, crowned with roses, lead the dance.'

To put down Richard, that sweet lovely rose
And plant this thorn, this canker, Bolingbroke.

And of the younger Caesar in *Antony and Cleopatra,* he causes Antony, enviously, to say, 'He wears the rose of youth upon him'; and in one of his finest Sonnets – the 35th, in which he excuses a friend's injury to him – Shakespeare uses the rose in a telling metaphor, again to symbolize everything perfect, or which at least would seem so:

Roses have thorns, and silver fountains mud;
Clouds and eclipses stain both moon and sun,
And loathsome canker lives in sweetest bud.
All men make faults...

And in the last, tragic act of *Othello,* when the distraught Moor, who, mad with jealousy, 'like the base Indian, threw a pearl away richer than all his tribe', kisses the sleeping Desdemona:

When I have pluck'd thy rose,
I cannot give it vital growth again,
It needs must wither: I'll smell it on the tree.

These are but six examples of Shakespeare mentioning the rose – there are over fifty others.

Writers in the East, and especially in Persia, the land of roses, were quick to weave the rose theme into their stories and legends. Sadi, the famous poet, called his celebrated book the *Gulistan* or Rose Garden, because, he writes, 'The Rose...may last at most four or five days, but my rose garden will blossom for ever.'

Yet another Persian poet, Nizami, one of the greatest of all, who wrote in the twelfth century his *Treasury of Mysteries,* tells a strange story in which a rose played an important and fatal part. It is a story of two rival physicians and a duel they fought, not with swords or daggers, but with poisons. First, one caused the other to swallow a lethal pill, but was frustrated by his opponent immediately taking an antidote which transformed the pill into something as innocuous as a sweetmeat. Then it was the other's turn. Taking a rose he appeared to cast a spell on it, and then asked the rival doctor to sniff it. No sooner had his opponent done so than he collapsed and died. Nizami goes to some lengths in his poem to explain that it was not magic that dealt death, but fear and the power of suggestion. The duel is depicted in the painting [figure 40] by an unknown painter who was one of Shah Tahmasp's retinue of artists, and probably painted it about 1550, three hundred years after the tale was written. Most Persian paintings are illustrations to manuscripts; and their extraordinary detail and clarity are partly due to the paper on

40 *The Duel of the Roses*, a Persian painting by one of Shah Tahmasp's court artists.

which they are painted, this being always prepared for the brush by being polished with an egg-shaped crystal.

Jewish folklore, too, has its rose story, and Sir John Mandeville, traveller and ostensible author of a book of largely imaginary voyages in the mid-fourteenth century, *Voiage and Travaile,* describes the origin of roses. A Jewish maid, it seems, Zillah, was once loved by a brutish sot named Hamuel. Zillah virtuously repels his advances, and so Hamuel accuses her of offences for which the penalty is death by burning; but when Zillah is brought to the stake the flames do her no harm, but reaching out, burn Hamuel to a cinder; then a further miracle occurs and the burning brands become red roses, and those that have not yet caught fire become white roses. These, according to the imaginative Sir John, were the first roses to bloom on earth since the loss of Paradise.

The plot of one of the favourite of all fairy stories, *Beauty and the Beast,* hinges on a rose. The best-known version of the story

41 A scene from *La Belle et la Bête,* Jean Cocteau's film of the well-known fairy story.

first appeared among the *Contes* of Madame de Villeneuve in 1744 and runs thus: A merchant, who has recently lost his money, leaves his daughters to go on a journey in the hopes of remaking his fortune. Each of his daughters, save Beauty, asks him to bring her back extravagant presents. Beauty asks only for a rose, 'only a rose, dear father'. The merchant departs and his journey is unsuccessful, but on his return he passes the garden of an apparently deserted castle. From it he cuts a rose for Beauty. But the castle is inhabited by a hideous monster, half man, half beast, who takes the merchant prisoner and says that he will kill him for stealing the rose, unless he gives him his daughter.

42, 43 Two illustrations by J. I. Grandville in *Les Fleurs Animées*, in which the single rose, Eglantine, is given the personality of a blue-stocking *(left)*, and the double rose *(right)* is the Queen of Flowers.

Beauty saves her father's life by going to the Beast's castle; gradually she is filled with pity for the Beast and comes to love him. When she finally consents to marry him, her love and bravery release him from a magic spell and he turns into a handsome prince.

America, too, has its rose legends. The most attractive is about the origin of the Cherokee rose, as told by Miss Jean Gordon in her book *Pageant of the Rose*. The Cherokee Indians, it appears, were once led by a brave and handsome warrior whose name was Tuswenahi. One day, when this warrior returned from a hunting trip which took him far from home, he found his settlement destroyed and his sweetheart, Dowansa, missing. His frantic search for her was ended when the Nunnshi, or little people, told him that in order to save her they had had to turn her into a white rose with golden breasts. The following spring found the maiden blooming in full purity, but she begged the little people to give her thorns to protect her against thoughtless people, including Tuswenahi himself, her lover, who carelessly trampled on her flowers. So the Nunnshi covered every stem with multitudinous prickles, so sharp that even animals do not dare to eat them.

There is a strange and rather sombre American legend about a rose, the Grant Rose. During the Seminole rising of 1835, Grant, an early settler in Florida, was returning home when he was attacked by the Indians. Having killed him, the Indians proceeded to his homestead where they found Mrs Grant and her child. Mrs Grant fled into the forest clutching her baby, but her full-skirted crinoline caught in the briars and brambles, and the Indians soon caught them and stabbed both mother and child to death. From the blood-soaked ground, it is said, sprang a rose tree bearing flowers the colour of blood – which are almost unique among roses in having a heavy, unpleasant odour.

The Germans have many legends of the rose. In one they say that in Pagan times the rose was dedicated to Freyja, the Venus of the Teutonic and Northern Countries, but with the advent of Christianity it became the Marienröschen of the Virgin Mary; for it is said that she once laid her veil on a rose bush to dry, and so all-pervading was her purity that thereafter the bush and its descendants bore none but white blossoms.

The rose, too, has always played important but different parts in the romantic 'Language of Flowers' in which many flowers and fruits have been given their own significance. A Rose Bud denotes a yet unawakened heart, a full blown Rose beauty that must pass, a red Rose ardour and a white Rose spiritual love.

In the seventeenth century in England the rose was generally acclaimed by poets, and by one in particular, who seems to have had a veritable passion for the flower, Herrick (1591–1674),

44 A nineteenth-century garland of roses and carnations in wrought iron by Servat, in the Musée des Arts Décoratifs in Paris.

45 'A rose-red city, half as old as time', was the description applied to Petra by John William Burgon.

who points out how short a life is that of a rose and urges immediate enjoyment of any offered pleasures:

> Gather ye Rose-buds while ye may,
> Old Time is still a-flying:
> And this same flower that smiles today,
> Tomorrow will be dying.

And it was Herrick who wrote a charming and little quoted poem about the death of the rose itself:

> The Rose was sick and smiling, died
> And (being to be sanctified)
> About the Bed, there sighing stood
> The sweet, and flowery Sisterhood.
> Some hung the head, while some did bring
> (To wash her) water from the Spring.
> Some laid her forth, while other wept,
> But all a solemn Fast there kept.
> The holy Sisters some among
> The sacred Dirge and Trentall sung.
> But ah! what sweets smelt every where,
> As Heaven had spent all perfumes there.
> At last, when prayers for the dead
> And Rites were all accomplishèd;
> They, weeping, spread a Lawney Loome,
> And closed her up, as in a Tombe.

And on another occasion:

> Roses at first were white
> Till they co'd not agree
> Whether my Sapho's breast
> Or they more white sho'd be.

The white rose that became red is a theme that writers and poets have always dallied with. Bion held that red roses sprang from the blood of Adonis. Lewis Carroll's card-gardeners painted white roses red to please the Queen of Hearts, and Oscar Wilde told the story of a rose dyed with the blood of a nightingale.

The association of the nightingale with the rose has been celebrated by the poets in many lands. There is an Eastern saying, 'You may place a hundred handfuls of fragrant herbs and flowers before the Nightingale; yet he wishes not, in his constant heart, for more than the sweet breath of his beloved Rose.'

Through the seventeenth century poets continued to sing the praises of the rose, and Marvell, with his own unique feeling for growing things, 'grass, fruit, the mossy root', boasts,

46 *The Madonna in the Rose Bower* by Bernardino Luini, 1365, in the Brera Gallery.

47 *(opposite)* The Victorian era was the heyday of the Valentine; typical is this example from the Victoria and Albert Museum, a profusion of roses with a sprig of forget-me-nots.

40

I have a Garden of my own
But so with Roses over-grown
And Lillies, that you would it guess
To be a little Wilderness.

Edmund Waller, the poet of the Restoration, asks the rose to help him in his love-making:

Go, lovely Rose –
Tell her that wastes her time and me,
That now she knows,
When I resemble her to thee,
How sweet and fair she seems to be.

In the eighteenth century poets were less concerned with the rose, though early in the nineteenth century Blake, Keats and Shelley all sang of it as the Queen of Flowers, and Blake, in one of his most quoted poems, describes it as being menaced by a very curious insect indeed, 'the invisible worm that flies in the night'. Keats loved roses, writing in gratitude to a friend:

But when, O Wells, thy roses came to me
My sense with their deliciousness was spell'd.
Soft voices had they, that with tender plea
Whispered of peace and truth and friendliness unquelled,

and asks nostalgically:

What is more tranquil than a musk rose blowing
In a green island, far from all men's knowing?

48 In *Alice in Wonderland*, illustrated by Sir John Tenniel, the gardeners painted white roses red to please the Queen of Hearts.

49 The romance of the nightingale and the rose was a favourite subject for Persian artists: a sixteenth-century embroidered panel.

Shelley, in one of his best-loved poems, heaped roses for his beloved's bed. Later the rose came really into its own, and Thomas Moore wrote the famous ballad of *The Last Rose of Summer*. Tennyson could hardly hear the sound made by falling rose petals; his roses waited for Maud in the garden; they stayed awake to see her. Matthew Arnold strewed on his love 'Roses, roses and never a spray of yew'.

In 1848, a few years after Redouté, 'Raphael of the Rose', died covered with honours, there was published in France an enchanting book which to this day is the joy of bibliophiles and flower lovers alike: *Les Fleurs Animées*. J. I. Grandville was famous for his caricatures of human weakness, pride, snobbishness and so on, which he portrayed in his illustrations of flowers, vegetables and animals, to which he delighted to give human characteristics, usually unflattering. In his *Human Flowers* there is an attractive illustration showing the Rose enthroned as Queen of Flowers [figure 43].

50 'Robin Redbreast's Cushion', according to an old country legend, will cure whooping-cough if tied round a child's neck.

51 ''Tis the last rose of summer
Left blooming alone
All her lovely companions
Are faded and gone.'
Thomas Moore (1779–1852).

Taxile Delord, in the entertaining text he wrote to accompany the illustrations, has a lot of mild fun to poke at the unfortunate Eglantine, said to be the flower of poets. In this satire on the literary hostesses of the day, it is difficult to imagine why the simple wild rose should be translated into the slightly ridiculous figure, 'the first of the blue stockings', whom Delord derides. She was, according to him, the patroness of every handsome young writer, and, 'as one name was not enough, she took the additional one of Clemence-Isaure'. But though an authoress herself, she seldom had the satisfaction of seeing her writing in print, because 'as newspapers had not been invented, Eglantine, now called Clemence-Isaure, did not have the joy of reading each morning the results of her inspiration of the day before'. She had to content herself with reading them to her friends at literary afternoons.

Eglantine's mania for literature and literary entertaining left her no time at all for household duties, which she came to relegate almost entirely to her unfortunate husband Lautrec, who had to cope with the cook, the laundry-maid, the butcher and other tradespeople. A child was born (one wonders how she ever found time to take the necessary steps) and poor Lautrec had to take entire care of it, Eglantine having made the delighted discovery that 'a husband is a nurse provided by the *Code civil*'.

Lautrec died, brought low by his household chores and unnatural nursery duties, and though Eglantine thought that it would be highly convenient to marry again at once (after all – who was to bath the baby?) none of Eglantine's young men felt inclined to take on the situation; so the unconsoled widow assuaged her loneliness by founding a school for poets, at which the prizes were to be an eglantine flower, in gold, and the favours of Eglantine herself; which was first prize and which second, we do not know; nor do we know the fate of the baby.

'Do not laugh at poor Eglantine,' says Delord patronizingly. 'She fulfilled and still fulfils, a useful purpose; for after all, what would become of misunderstood poets without the sympathy of the blue-stocking?'

Later in the century roses are found to play a part in both of Lewis Carroll's famous 'Alice' books; in *Alice in Wonderland* Alice finds the card-gardeners desperately trying to paint the white roses red, and in *Through the Looking Glass* roses take a disagreeably human quality when they engage poor Alice in conversation – far from politely:

''It's *my* opinion that you never think *at all*'', the Rose said in a rather severe tone.
''I never saw anything that looked stupider'', a Violet said, so suddenly that Alice quite jumped, for it hadn't spoken before.
''Hold your tongue''! cried the Tiger-lily. ''As if you ever saw

anybody! You keep your head under your leaves and snore away there, till you know no more what's going on in the world, than if you were a bud!''

''Are there many people in the garden besides me?'' Alice said, not choosing to notice the Rose's last remark.

''There's one other flower in the garden that can move about like you,'' said the Rose, ''I wonder how you do it – '' (''You're always wondering'', said the Tiger-lily), ''but she's more bushy than you are.''

52   In 1867 the introduction of the first Hybrid Tea rose *La France* was followed by the appearance of many hybrids, among them this sweetly-scented *Baronne de Rothschild*, a rose now seldom grown.

53 *Rosa sulfurea*, painted by Redouté, has been in cultivation since 1625 or earlier; until the introduction of *Rosa foetida persiana*, it was the only large double yellow rose.

"Is she like me?" Alice asked eagerly, for the thought crossed her mind, "There's another little girl in the garden, some-where!"

"Well, she has the same awkward shape as you", the Rose said, "but she's redder — and her petals are shorter, I think."

"Her petals are done up close, almost like a dahlia," the Tiger-lily interrupted: "not tumbled about anyhow, like yours."

"But that's not *your* fault", the Rose added, "you're beginning to fade you know – and then one can't help one's petals getting a little untidy."

Twenty-five years later Oscar Wilde, in one of his best-loved stories, wrote a tale full of gentleness and compassion, of the nightingale and the rose; a young student, passionately in love, is told by his wayward sweetheart that she will only dance with him and listen to his declarations if he brings her a red rose. In all his garden there is no red rose, so the student is cast down, and complains bitterly of his misfortune. A nightingale, 'from her nest in the holm oak tree' overhears him, takes pity on him, and offers to try to find him the rose he needs. But all the rose trees round about seem only to bear white roses 'white as the foam of the sea' or yellow roses, 'yellow as the hair of the mermaiden who sits on an amber throne'. At last the nightingale does find a red rose tree but all its blooms have been killed by frost and again the nightingale is disappointed and cries, 'One red rose is all I want – only one red rose. Is there no way by which I can get it?' 'There is a way,' said the tree, 'but it is so terrible that I dare not tell it to you.' 'Tell it to me,' said the nightingale. 'I am not afraid.' 'If you want a red rose,' said the tree, 'you must build it out of music by moonlight, and stain it with your own heart's blood. You must sing to me with your breast against a thorn. All night long you must sing to me and the thorn must pierce your heart, and your life blood must flow into my veins and become mine.' 'Death is a great price to pay for a red rose,' cried the nightingale, 'and life is very dear to all. It is pleasant to sit in the green wood and to watch the sun in his chariot of gold, and the moon in her chariot of pearl. Sweet is the scent of the hawthorn, and sweet are the bluebells that hide in the valley, and the heather that blows on the hill. Yet love is better than life, and what is the heart of a bird compared to the

54 'It was roses, roses all the way'; surely this is one of the most familiar of English quotations, but how many people know how it goes on, or what Browning was writing about?

'It was roses, roses all the way,
With myrtle mixed in my path like mad.
The house-roofs seemed to heave and sway,
The church-spires flamed, such flags they had,
A year ago on this very day!'

Browning wrote *The Patriot* in 1849 when he was in Italy, an interested and sympathetic observer of Italian efforts to shake off the Austrian yoke. The poem reflects the changing loyalties of the time, and how from one year to another a popular leader could lose his following, be denounced and even executed, like Arnold of Brescia who inspired this well-known poem.

heart of a man?' So the pact is made, and the nightingale sacrifices her life to bring the love-sick student his rose. But when the student offers his love the rose, she spurns it, saying that she prefers jewels, so the student throws the flower angrily away; but the nightingale lies dead in the long grass.

Writing some years ago, two English poets seem to be as against modern roses as many people are today, when we read of Christina Rossetti regretting the roses she remembered:

> Oh lost green paradise,
> Were the roses redder there
> Than they blossom other where?

And George Moore pontificating:

> The rose of the past is better
> Than the rose we ravish today;
> 'Tis holier, purer and fitter
> To place on the shrine where we pray,
> For the secret thoughts we obey.

With George Moore we reach our own century, when a great American writer, Gertrude Stein, wrote a line about a rose which will always be quoted 'Rose is a rose is a rose'. The words occur in her poem *Sacred Emily*, and when Gertrude Stein wrote it, the rose had come to mean almost everything else except a rose. It meant beauty, bravery and suffering; in fact it had assumed as many meanings as poets had wanted it to do. It was a woman's lips, a beloved's cheek, but not a flower any more. 'Rose is a rose' – the line that is familiar to everyone, even to those who have never heard of Gertrude Stein – reaffirms the simple, but apt-to-be-forgotten fact; and the poet herself had it printed in a circle and made it her symbol. As we repeat the straightforward, unarguable phrase it becomes a kind of credo – an expression of faith. Rhythmic and gentle, the words come to conjure for us the scent, the colour and the form of the rose itself.

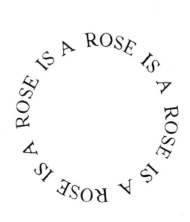

55 Alice, in *Through the Looking Glass*, has a long conversation with the flowers.

48

THE ROSE IN ART

THE ROSE IN ART makes a tardy appearance – we look in vain for it in Greece, except in a highly stylized and hardly recognizable form. In Roman days, in the decorative arabesques which decorated the houses of Herculaneum and Pompeii, flowers do play their part – but it would be difficult to recognize any particular one. Roses, unlike the iris and the lotus, do not figure in the frescoes and wall paintings of Egypt. Clumsy representations of flowers – five petals round a boss of stamens, which might as well be a buttercup as a single rose – do appear in early sculpture, but we have to turn the pages of history quite a way before we come to a true representation of an undoubted rose.

An early example is the triumphant red rose which depicts the heroine of the *Romaunt de la Rose* [figure 7]. From the fourteenth century onwards roses used as incidental decoration are to be found in every form – painted, woven, carved and later printed [figure 56]. Gradually the aim of the flower artist changed, from merely recording the structure of flowers, to creating the finished works of art which flower paintings ultimately became. The first down-to-earth, botanically correct, portraits of plants, flowers and roots, were those that appeared in the first medicine books and herbals. Informative and useful, but unlovely. Gradually with the years, this changed, and the artist was to give full rein to his own creative genius, and allow his eye to appreciate, and his hand to record the flower's real beauty. Mere diagrammatic illustrations become pictures.

One of the first of these real flower artists was Jacques de la Moyne, who painted the touchingly simple picture of a rose shown in figure 56.

Later, in the sixteenth and seventeenth centuries, the simple woodcuts of the first herbals gave place, in Holland especially, to great vases of tumbling luscious flowers, such as those painted by Van Huysam (1682–1749). But even before Van Huysam, a countryman of his, Bosschaert, appreciated the value of roses as models *per se*, and painted some of his loveliest pictures of roses alone [figure 60].

Lovely and famous women, of course, were continually painted with roses, the flowers' transient beauty pointing a moral as well as adorning the canvas; Diane de Poitiers, Mary Queen of Scots, the beauties of Charles II's court and Marie Antoinette [figure 65] being just a few.

57 A drawing by Jean Cocteau, autographed by himself and by Nijinsky, the creator of the role of *Le Spectre de la Rose*, now in the collection of Lady Juliet Duff.

56 *(opposite)* A single rose painted by one of the earliest flower artists, Jacques de La Moyne de Morgues, who lived in the sixteenth century. A Huguenot, de Morgues went as cartographer on an expedition to Florida, and eventually, after the massacre of St Bartholomew, settled in England.

58 Carl Fabergé, the celebrated Russian jeweller, devised this clock in the form of a rose: the dial is enclosed in diamonds.

By the eighteenth·century there were innumerable flower paintings. Even Guardi, famed for his Venetian scenes, painted flower pictures, and he was soon followed by the greatest flower painter of them all, Redouté, of whom more later. Nearer our own day Renoir painted the roses he grew at Cagnes, while Monet painted several groups in rose gardens [figure 72]. Art Nouveau welcomed the rose as an art form and twisted and converted its graceful shape in many ways, using it to decorate furniture, lamps and even the notices for the Paris Métro. Douanier Rousseau found the rose, as so many before him, the ultimate emblem of beauty. Only the Cubists, afraid, perhaps, of the rose's very perfection, hesitated to paint it.

And yet, though through the centuries the rose has continually been the subject (alone or with other flowers) for the artist's brush, the name we shall always connect with rose painting is Redouté.

O peintre aimé de Flore et du riant Empire
Tu nous quittes le jour où le printemps expire.

'It was June, of the year 1840,' writes Miss Eva Mannering in her introduction to *Pierre Joseph Redouté: Roses.* 'An old man of eighty had died, and on his coffin was laid a wreath of roses

59 Detail from an early German painting of *The Virgin with a Rose Branch*, School of Schongauer, in the Museum at Strasbourg.

and lilies bearing the inscription quoted above. It was a fitting epitaph. For Pierre Joseph Redouté, that most prolific and popular of botanical artists, had, during his long and industrious working life, caught and preserved the essence of bygone Spring and Summer days in his meticulous flower paintings. And whilst, in the capacity of illustrator of botanical books, his attention had been focussed on a multitude of flowers and plants, he loved best and best recorded the infinitely varied beauty of roses and lilies.'

60 Detail from a still-life by one of the first flower artists, Johannes Bosschaert, who worked between 1626 and 1643.

61 A rose from the collection of Her Majesty the Queen, made by Fabergé of crystal, gold, enamel and diamonds.

63 These Battersea boxes, used either for comfits or snuff, were made in the shape of roses in 1750.

62 An eighteenth-century French rose watch in pink enamel and gold.

64 An ink-pot of Coalport china, made in the shape of a rose in about 1830.

Pierre Joseph Redouté was born in Luxembourg in the year that British soldiers went into battle wearing roses in their caps at Minden, 1759. His family had always been painters, and while still a boy he made a journey through the Low Countries to study the paintings of the great Dutch masters. When he was twenty-three he went to Paris, and after some years when he worked at stage design, by a fortunate chance he met the rich botanist Charles de Brutelle. Already Redouté was fascinated by flowers,

53

65 Queen Marie Antoinette *en gaule* (as a peasant), a portrait which caused a storm of protest when Vigée le Brun painted it, for it was considered that the Queen was not grandly enough dressed.

and de Brutelle was to encourage him to make flower-painting his career, and sent him to England to study the plants at Kew. While in England something of the greatest importance to his career occurred: he had the opportunity of studying the art of stipple engraving, which was to play such an important part in printing the flower portraits which were to make him famous.

On his return to Paris, Redouté made the acquaintance of Gerard van Spaëndonck, whose *Fleurs dessinées après nature* are some of the most beautiful of all flower engravings. Van

67 A golden rose tree such as the Pope used to send as a token of regard to worthy Catholic sovereigns of Europe, made for Pius II in 1459.

66 Pierre Joseph Redouté, most famous of all rose portraitists (1759–1840).

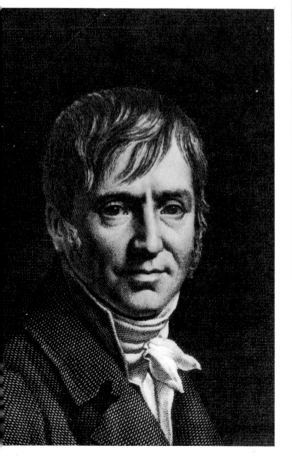

Spaëndonck was quick to recognize Redouté's genius and gave him an appointment on the Royal Collections of Paintings on Vellum. Soon after, another important appointment came Redouté's way, that of drawing-master to Queen Marie Antoinette, and in that capacity, he visited the Queen in prison in the Temple, bringing her drawings he had made of plants, and sometimes the plants themselves. But, as we have seen, it was the wife of the next ruler of France, Joséphine de Beauharnais, who was to be his greatest and most munificent Royal patron.

With the Empire, Redouté's great days had come. Protected and encouraged by the Empress, to whom one of his greatest works, *Les Liliacées*, was dedicated, he worked on the volumes which were to make his name immortal in the world of flowers and flower-lovers, *Les Roses*, published in 1817, two years after Waterloo. Other books followed, all equally successful and sought after, but it is on his rose illustrations that Redouté's fame most surely rests.

68 Oliver Messel, the celebrated stage-designer, devised this rose, sparkling in silver and diamanté, for a production of Richard Strauss' *Der Rosenkavalier* at Glyndebourne.

69 A jug of Derby china, *c*. 1800. At this time the Derby factory employed 'Pegg the Quaker', a talented flower artist who decorated many of their finest pieces.

The rose being the most beautiful of flowers, it was, of course, often counterfeited in jewels and in gold, and William Prescott, the American historian, in his great work *The Conquest of Peru* describes how, such was the natural wealth of their country, the Incas, as well as planting gardens where every sort of vegetable and flower grew and flourished, set 'parterres of a more extraordinary kind,... glowing with the various forms of vegetable life skilfully imitated in gold...' After the imprisonment by the Spaniards of the King of the Incas, the distraught ruler offered what must surely be the largest ransom in history for his liberty: a room twenty-two feet long and seventeen feet

70 The Polish mezzo-soprano Maria Olczewska as Oktavian in Strauss' *Der Rosenkavalier*.

71 A photograph by Baron de Meyer, one of the greatest of photographers, of Nijinsky as *Le Spectre de la Rose* in 1912.

broad, completely filled with gold to a height as high as the Inca – a tall man – could reach. Pizarro, the rapacious leader of the Spaniards, agreed, and at once golden objects, the famous golden flowers among them, poured into the capital from the farthest parts of Peru, offered loyally by the natives to ransom their sovereign. Finally a mass of gold, worth, when Prescott wrote (in 1847), over three million pounds, and by now immeasurably more, was accumulated and handed over. But the Spaniards, with a cruelty and lack of faith of which history offers few parallels, took the gold but killed the Inca shortly after the ransom was completed. Ironically, the unhappy ruler was treated like a monarch to the last and, though chained, was led to execution wearing his royal crown, the 'borla' and ceremonial cloak of bat's skin. So died the Inca, and the ransom gold, cups, coronets, bracelets and breast plates, and the golden roses, were melted into ingots and shipped to Spain.

Golden roses played a very different part in connection with the Roman Catholic Church, when it was the custom for the Pope to bless a golden rose and send it to the sovereign of some Roman Catholic power as a token of esteem. The Holy Father would send with it this message: 'Accept this rose at our hand who, albeit unworthy, holds the place of God on earth, by which rose is typified the joy of the heavenly Jerusalem and of the Church Militant by which to all the faithful in Christ is manifested that most beauteous flower, which is the joy and crown of all saints. Receive, then, thou dearly beloved son, who art, according to the age, noble, potent, and endowed with many virtues, that thou mayest be more fully enobled with every virtue in Christ our Lord, as a rose planted by the streams of many waters.' Henry VIII was the last English monarch to receive this distinction. The rose, delicate and ephemeral, was emblematic of the frailty of the body and the shortness of human life. The precious and unchanging metal of which it was modelled alluded to the immortality of the soul.

Such a golden rose was sent by Pope Pius IX to the Empress Eugénie of France, and as the Empress was devoutly religious this tribute from the Pope at once became her proudest possession. After the fall of the Second Empire and the burning of the Tuileries during the Commune, the Empress thought her precious rose was lost for ever. Some years later, however, an anonymous parcel was delivered at her home in exile at Chislehurst which, when opened, was found to contain the rose which someone must have salvaged from the ruins of the Tuileries; and the Empress kept it by her till the day of her death nearly fifty years later.

Roses have ever been prized models for the jeweller. Benvenuto Cellini (1500–71) fashioned roses in enamel, gold and pearls and harnessed his jewelled mermaids and sea monsters

72 Women in a rose garden, painted by Claude Monet in the last sunlit years of the Second Empire. Claude Monet (1840–1926), a founder of the Impressionist school of painting, had great feeling for painting flowers and gardens.

73 Diane de Poitiers, mistress of King Henry II of France, in her bath; possibly by Clouet, *c.* 1520.

with traces made of roses. One of Queen Elizabeth's suitors, the Duc d'Alençon (her 'Little Frog') tried to win the cold Queen's heart with gifts of splendid jewels, among them a rose in white enamel with a butterfly of rubies and sapphires, and on New Year's Day, 1571, one of the Queen's most elaborate presents was an ornament made of the white rose of York surrounded by the red roses of Lancaster in enamel and rubies. What better offering to one of whom the poet Fulke Greville had written:

> Under a throne I saw a virgin sit,
> The red and white rose quartered in her face.

In the eighteenth century jewellers delighted to create ornaments of diamonds in the form of rose wreaths and garlands. Some were made with hidden springs which caused the jewelled flowers to nod and tremble as the wearer moved, like the magnificent necklace shown on figure 77, once the property of that great collector of Victoriana, Lady Cory.

When Lady Cory was collecting and wearing her famous jewels in Edwardian days, there was a jeweller, the favourite of every European court, whose work, more than that of any other similar craftsman, epitomizes his own time, Carl Fabergé, the son of a Swiss immigrant to Russia.

Today his work commands enormous prices and is to be found in museums the world over. Fabergé was the favourite jeweller of the Tsars, and every year, especially at Easter and Christmas, he would supply the Imperial Family with presents for them to exchange. The Easter eggs he made are legendary and must have cost hundreds, if not thousands of pounds. His cigarette cases are classic in their simplicity of design, and his animals are brilliantly carved and fascinating in the way they interpret simple humour, farmyard fun, in rare stones and exotic minerals: a pig in rhodonite, for instance, or an owl in orlets quartz. But it is in his flowers that Fabergé manifests his true genius. H.C. Bainbridge, in his life of Carl Fabergé, rightly says, 'However... you may play tricks with animals, you cannot be funny with flowers. They are the perfection of all created things. Absolute aristocrats, you cannot subordinate them: they will do nothing for you except in their own sweet way... and if you would represent them, you must do so petal for petal, pistil by pistil, and leaf for leaf. You must take no liberties...'. Fabergé's Easter eggs, with their secret springs, jewelled peacocks, and unfolding Imperial miniatures, may be described as ostentatious and sentimental, his animals dismissed as comic trifles, his cigarette cases as ridiculously expensive and rather heavy; but his flowers, with their exquisite workmanship and respect for nature, must surely be recognized as artistic works of a high order [figure 58].

74 John James Audubon (1780–1851), the great American ornithologist and painter of birds, combined American flora and fauna in his print of the Carolina rose and the seaside finch.

The age of Fabergé was also the age of Richard Strauss, whose opera *Der Rosenkavalier* is a shining celebration of the rose, this time in music. This was first performed in Dresden in 1911. At once its lilting, nostalgic (though anachronistic) waltz music cast a spell on opera-lovers the world over. Its bitter-sweet Viennese charm, a mixture of sentiment and cynicism and almost Proustian preoccupation with time and the changes it brings, *Die Zeit ist wie eine Uhr*, has made it the most loved of all Strauss' operas. But in the shimmering opening of the second act,

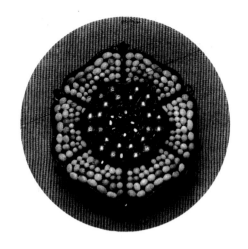

The Presentation of the Rose, all is youth and simplicity and love.

Oktavian's servants enter in their liveries of white and pale green... Footmen-heyducks with crescent-shaped Hungarian sabres – lackeys in soft white leather and green ostrich feathers. They are followed by a Negro, who carries the rose's case. Finally Oktavian, carrying in his right hand the rose. He approaches Sophie with an air of importance, but his boyish face is blushing and shy. His extreme good looks, and her own excitement make Sophie grow pale. They look at each other, and their beauty and mutual embarrassment increase their shyness.

OKTAVIAN: I have the honour, in the name of my noble cousin Von Lerchenau, to present the rose of love to his bride.

SOPHIE: I am grateful to my lord...
Smelling the rose...
It has a strong scent . . . like a real rose.

OKTAVIAN: There is Persian attar in it.

SOPHIE: It is like a rose from Paradise... Do you not think so, too?
Oktavian bows over the rose, and then looks up at Sophie, who says,

SOPHIE: It is like a greeting from Heaven... unbearably sweet,

And then she says softly,

SOPHIE: It tugs my heart strings.

75, 76 *(above)* A Victorian version of the Tudor rose, in turquoises with a jewelled centre. *(below)* In 1829 the Emperor Pedro of Brazil was forced by his Government into marriage with a German princess. The Emperor awaited his unseen bride with great misgivings, but was enchanted to find that Princess Amalia was a delightful beauty. In her honour he founded the Order of the Rose, whose motto, *Amor e Fidelidade,* appears on the badge.

78 Recently the well-known firm of jewellers, Tiffany of New York, have revived the art of *vermeil*, producing beautiful objects such as this.

Then, in chorus, the enchanting young pair, newly fallen in love, sing of the unbelievable happiness which has, suddenly, enfolded them. There have been many Rosenkavaliers – but few have looked so fascinating as Olzewska who sang in a legendary production with Lotte Lehmann as the Marschallin and Elizabeth Schumann as Sophie.

Contemporary with *Der Rosenkavalier*, was another great artistic event with a rose as its central motif, this time a ballet. Though many artists have given roses human characteristics, never in any art form has a rose come to life so dramatically as in the ballet *Le Spectre de la Rose*. This was inspired by Théophile Gautier's poem, and became one of the great choreographer Fokine's most famous compositions.

A girl, coming home from her first ball, lies back in a chair and dreamingly thinks of the evening she has just passed, and especially of one handsome partner with whom she danced. In her hand she holds the rose he gave her. Smelling it, and tired out by the pleasure of the ball, she falls asleep, and at once the Spirit of the Rose, a gauzy mysterious figure in no way human, enters, as if a vapour of the night. Not a man, not a rose. A thought perhaps? Or a promise? With one leap he crosses the stage, gently wakes the girl who finds in the slender gentle Spirit of the Rose her half formed dreams of love come true. They dance together and the girl recaptures something of the happiness of the ball, and with it a foretaste of all that romantic love can offer. Sinking once more into her chair she falls asleep, and the Spirit of the Rose, with one breathtaking bound, leaps through the window, into the rose scented night, and away.

Such was the *Spectre de la Rose*, Nijinsky's most famous ballet; and his celebrated last leap, when he sailed in a single bound out through the window, became the sensation of Europe and America. So much indeed was it discussed, that his other transcendent qualities as a ballet dancer were forgotten. He would be irritated by this and say, 'I am not only a jumper. I am an artist too.' Some people even suspected him of having springs concealed in his shoes.

Bakst himself designed the original costume for Nijinsky as the Spirit of the Rose, and he took infinite care that each rose petal, in all their different shaded pinks, lavenders and roses, should be cut differently. The costume took the form of a close-fitting sweater of silk elastic; this covered Nijinsky's entire body except his chest and arms, which were encircled with armlets of rose petals, so that some of the petals should appear half faded, others crisp and curling. They were curled with hot tongs before each appearance.

77 *(opposite)* A magnificent diamond spray from the collection of Victorian jewellery bequeathed to the Victoria and Albert Museum by Lady Cory.

THE ORIGIN OF THE ROSE

No one knows
Through what wild centuries
Roves back the Rose.

So WROTE WALTER DE LA MARE; and if you delve into the past to try to discover something about the origin, history and relationship of garden roses, you will realize how true his words are.

Broadly speaking, roses stem from several shoots, some with their origin in China and the Middle East, others from the shores of the Mediterranean, others in North America. The greatest contribution to the birth and development of modern roses has undoubtedly been made by the China rose (*R. chinensis*) and its close relative the Tea rose (*R. odorata*), both of which probably sprang from the same unknown stock. Both of these roses are comparatively recent comers to European gardens, the former arriving from the East early in the eighteenth century and the latter a century later; but both are old in Chinese history and art, and were grown and developed there for centuries before their descendants reached us.

From *R. chinensis* came the Bourbon rose, a cross, so it is believed, between it and the *Rose de Quatre Saisons*, a variety of the Damask rose (*R. damascena*), another 'child' of *R. chinensis* (this time by *R. moschata*). This later came to play its part in the creation of the Hybrid Musks and some of the Wichuriana ramblers as a result of crossing with the latter. To *Rosa chinensis* also, in its form called *R. minima*, we owe the group of miniature roses which recently, and rightly, have become so popular.

At the same time as the Chinese were developing *R. chinensis*, it is not unreasonable to suppose that similar activities were taking place in Europe; and *R. gallica*, a species now widely spread throughout Europe, Western Asia and North America, but thought to have had its origin in ancient Gaul, is generally believed to be the prototype of the group of 'Old Roses' embracing the Cabbage rose (*R. centifolia*) and its offspring the Moss rose (*R. centifolia muscosa*) [figure 80], the Damask rose (*R. damascena*) and the York rose (*R. alba*). Whatever their origin, and whether they are species or hybrids, authorities are still not agreed, but both the Cabbage and the Damask roses do have certain affinities with *R. gallica*, while *R. alba*, often called the Jacobite rose, is generally thought to be a result of a union

79 *(opposite) Rosa bourboniana* was the product of an accidental crossing of a China and a Damask rose in the French island of Réunion, where they were used for hedging.

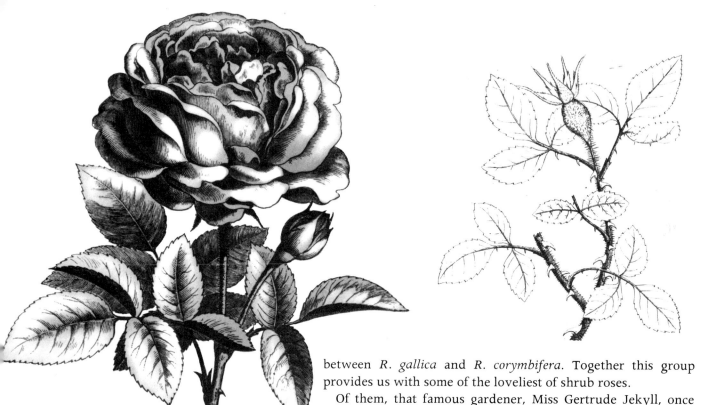

80, 81 *(left) Rosa centifolia*, the rose with a hundred petals; *(right) Rosa sinica hystrix*, remarkable for its bristly hips and sepals.

82 *Rosa indica odoratissima*, which has tightly folded crimson petals and highly polished foliage

between *R. gallica* and *R. corymbifera*. Together this group provides us with some of the loveliest of shrub roses.

Of them, that famous gardener, Miss Gertrude Jekyll, once wrote:

'These were the roses that so often appear in the pictures of the Dutch flower painters; and in more recent years it was these flowers, now old-fashioned but always adorable, that, amid all the thousands of more modern kinds, held the admiration and inspired some of the most beautiful work of Fantin-Latour, whose genius and sympathy enabled him to show on his canvases not only their intrinsic beauty and dignity, but a pathetic suggestion of their relation to human life and happiness.'

Another wonderful race of roses, *Rosa rugosa,* hails from Japan, and was known there (and also in China) a thousand years ago, but it has played comparatively little part in modern rose development, largely because it is not a particularly good mixer. As a result, it has yielded few varieties, although some of its hybrids like Mrs Anthony Waterer, *Parfum de l'Hay,* the exquisite *Blanc double de Coubert* and the lovely, creamy Agnes, are useful and valuable plants, as much for their brilliant yellow autumn foliage and rich fruit as for their flowers.

Whether or not they stem from a common stock originally, the Austrian rose (*R. foetida*) [figure 17] and the Scotch rose (*R. spinosissima*) would seem to be closely related. From a variety of the former, *R. foetida persiana,* the Persian Yellow rose, came the first Pernetiana rose and as a result of a historical marriage with a Hybrid Perpetual, sprang the whole race of Hybrid Pernetianas with all their distinctive tones of orange, apricot and yellow. A hundred and fifty years ago, *R. spinosis-*

66

sima proved a fertile field for the rose breeder, but after a period, interest lapsed for some reason and it was not until comparatively recently that some modern breeders – Herr Kordes from Germany, in particular – have turned to this species once again, crossing it with various Hybrid Tea varieties to give us such fine shrub roses as Frühlingsgold, with creamy, gold-centred flowers and a delicious wild rose scent, and the single, pink-edged, crimson-stamened Frühlingsmorgen.

The first Polyanthas, now so popular, came from a cross between *R. chinensis* and *R. multiflora*; later, these were to be infused with the blood of the Tea Rose and still later with the blood of Teas and Bourbons, Hybrid Perpetuals and Hybrid Teas, to give us the now familiar galaxy of Hybrid Polyanthas or Floribundas. Our modern roses have come a long way from their starting point, and we have reaped rich rewards from the original rather insignificant roses of two and three centuries ago: this is entirely thanks to the patient labours of keen growers and breeders in many lands. And the good work still goes on – to give us healthier and more sweetly scented roses every year.

Each part, each colour, each kind of the rose has always had its own special appeal to different rose lovers. Sir Thomas Browne, the seventeenth-century doctor and botanist, whose work *The Garden of Cyrus* was published in 1658, was particularly fascinated by the sepals, the green leaflets which spring from above the hip and enclose the bud: of these he writes:

'Nothing is more admired than the five brethren of the Rose, and the strange disposure of the appendices or beards on the calycular leaves thereof . . . For those two that are smooth and of no beard, are contrived to be undermost, as without prominent parts, and fit to be smoothly covered, the other two which are beset with beards on either side stand outwards and uncovered, but the fifth or half-bearded leaf is covered on the one side, but on the open side stands free and bearded like the other'.

And it is true that the sepals of the rose can be of great interest, even to the most amateurish botanist, for they often provide the clue in tracing a rose's ancestry. An example of this is to be found in the ordinary flower of the hedgerows, the Dog Rose. This rose, and all its descendants, have three different patterns of sepals, two bearded or fimbriated, two smooth-edged, and the fifth has one edge smooth and the other whiskered.

All gardeners, I suppose, have a moment in their lives which they may or may not remember, when the full fascination of botany and plants is suddenly realized. I experienced such a moment when Dr Luxmoore, the famous Eton master, then in his eighties, explained to me this curious sepal formation of the Dog Rose, on a warm Sunday evening in his garden on an island in the Thames. He took a rose bud and showed me the odd shapes of its five sepals, illustrating his words with a Latin phrase:

83 Roses have always played a part in human adornment: in this pen-and-ink sketch by Coypel (1694–1752) they festoon the costume of an appealing actress.

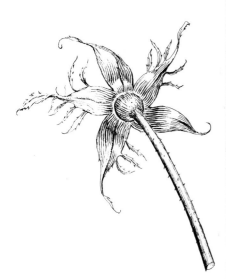

84 The oddly formed sepals of the Dog Rose, *Rosa canina*, and its descendants, known as 'The Five Brethren of the Rose'.

85 *Rosa cristata*: most of the fragrance of a Moss rose is secreted in its elaborate sepals, and if dried or pressed it retains its sweetness for years.

Quinque sumus fratres, et eodem tempore nati.
Sunt duo barbati. Duo sunt sine barba creati.
Unus et e quinque non est barbatus utrinque.

This little riddle might be loosely translated, perhaps, as follows:

Of us five brothers at the same time born,
Two from our birthday ever beards have worn.

86 Star of Waltham, as warm and comfortable as a Victorian afternoon in summer. It is seldom grown today.

On other two none ever have appeared,
While our fifth brother wears but half a beard.

Ruskin had his own reasons for the popularity throughout the ages of the rose, and more especially the red rose. He says:
'Perhaps few people have ever asked themselves why they admire the rose so much, more than all other flowers. If they consider, they will find, first that red is, in a delicately graduated state, the loveliest of all pure colours, and secondly, there is in

87 *Rosa chinensis*, from which many of our modern roses descend.

the rose no shadow except that which is composed of colour. All its shadows are fuller in colour than its lights, owing to the translucency and reflective powers of its leaves.'

Such red roses in our catalogues today are the beautiful heraldic *Rose moyesii*, the deep rich Hybrid Tea Charles Mallerin and the full and quartered Floribunda rose, Rosemary.

The Hybrid Tea White Wings is a beautiful single rose, with long, slender buds which open to five inch white single flowers, centred with a boss of golden stamens: and others are the climbing Sinica Anemone, silvery pink and flowering early, and the golden and glorious Mermaid.

Miss Gertrude Jekyll, one of the great gardeners of our century, loved sweet briars, and would urge her friends to plant hedges of them, for the sweet scent that their branches and

88 A country arrangement of briar blossoms and cabbage roses by Cecil Beaton.

leaves, let alone flowers, lay on the air after a shower. She writes:

'The next briar to bloom is the double pink, with the strong, sweet, luscious scent; the perfect rose scent, the true attar. This little flower seems to carry me back through the lifetime of past generations and to put me, in friendliest fashion, in touch with the flower lovers of them all. For to me it bears in its tender, half-opened blossoms with their dainty, rosy depths, and sweetest perfume, the whole sentiment of the deeply rooted English love of flower beauty and present enjoyment of garden delight.'

The briars, with their wild rose flowers and arching sprays, are among the loveliest unspoilt beauties of the garden. Of particular beauty are roses like *R. farreri persetosa*, with pink, minute coin-like flowers, and *R. rubrifolia*, with garnet-coloured leaves. *Rosa hugonis*, a briar rose with feathery leaves and yellow flowers, was named for Father Hugh Scallon, a missionary who botanized in West China in the last century.

ROSE GARDENS

ONE OF THE EARLIEST pictures of a rose garden – though a charmingly improbable one – is of a castle with its battlements planted with roses, shown in one of the illuminated illustrations to the *Romaunt de la Rose* in the British Museum [figure 7]. The garden in which Shakespeare sets his famous Wars of the Roses scene (see page 8) is not mentioned specially as being a rose garden, but simply as the Temple Garden. Francis Bacon, in his celebrated essay *Of Gardens,* in which he describes the various parts of a garden and how each should be planted, does not include a garden, set apart for roses; nor do eighteenth-century books on horticulture suggest that roses should be grown in a garden of their own. The Empress Joséphine, who wanted to grow every known variety of rose, was probably the first gardener to devote a whole garden to roses, and roses alone.

It was with the advent of all the new roses in the nineteenth century, and especially the introduction of the first Hybrid Teas, that rose gardens, as we think of them, became the fashion, even though in Alice's Looking Glass garden roses were still grown in a border with other flowers in 1872, the year when the book first appeared.

But by the eighties of the last century, rose gardens had become very elaborate, specialized affairs, pompous parterres of complicated beds cut out of turf, housing hundreds of Hybrid Tea roses, which were quite bare and flowerless for many months of the year and far from beautiful, while another innovation of this period was the standard rose, whose prim shape appealed greatly to the Victorian eye. This was the sort of rose growing that incurred the disapproval of that great gardener, William Robinson, who, with Miss Gertrude Jekyll, did much to create our concept of modern gardening. He wrote of rose gardens in 1883:

'There is great loss to the flower garden from the usual way of growing the rose as a thing apart, and its absence at present from the majority of flower gardens. It is surprising to see how poor and hard many places are to which the beauty of the rose might add delight, and the only compensation for all this blank is what they call the rosery, which in large places is often an ugly thing with plants that usually only blossom for a few weeks in summer. This idea of the rose garden arose when we had a much smaller number of roses, that flowered in summer mainly.'

90 *La Bouquetière,* a nineteenth-century French drawing of a rose-seller in the Paris streets.

89 *(opposite)* Perfection in pink: floribunda Lilac Charm.

73

91 A Victorian design for a rose garden.

92 Standard roses, with Hybrid Tea roses grown at their base.

This was nearly eighty years ago and how much truer today, when the choice of roses and the types of rose plants is so enormously increased. William Robinson went on to say:

The Rose is not only "decorative" but is the queen of all decorative plants, not in one sort of position or garden, but in many – not in one race or sort, but in many…' and he went on to plead they should be brought back into the garden proper, 'not only in beds, but in the old way – over bower and trellis and as bushes where they are hardy enough to stand our winters, so as to break up flat surfaces and give us light and shade where all is usually so level and hard. But the rose must not come back in ugly ways, in roses stuck – and mostly starving – on the tops of sticks or standards, or set in raw beds of manure, and pruned hard and set thin so as to develop large blooms; but as the bloom is beautiful in all stages and sizes, roses should be seen closely massed, feathering to the ground.'

Robinson's idea of how a rose garden should be planted is oddly modern, though his suggestions were only followed by very few for many years. But today, the Victorian and Edwardian rose garden, with its serried rows of Hybrid Tea roses in stiff geometrical beds, is a thing of the past. Modern rose gardens are planted with every kind of rose, with climbers on the walls, ramblers wreathing and festooning pillars and arches, and shrub roses making flowery hedges all about. Among such rose gardens are the great American rose gardens at Hartford, Connecticut and Hershey, Pennsylvania, the one in the Parco del Ouest in Madrid, which is called the Rosaleda [figure 94], the beautiful rose garden at Russborough in Ireland, the Bagatelle in Paris, and La Roseraie de l'Hay.

In the Rosaleda, roses seem to colour the air with their scent in May. All are grown to perfection, for there is something in the thin granite soil of that part of Spain which seems especially to suit them. This Spanish rose garden is a glorious sight, with its pergolas and tunnels of roses.

From the dry heat of Madrid to the damp coolness of County Wicklow. There, but nearly two months later, flowers a rose garden almost as beautiful as anywhere in Europe. At Russborough, a great Georgian house, acquired in 1951 by Sir Alfred and Lady Beit, there is a wonderful rose garden; and one where all the principles of William Robinson have, one feels, consciously been followed. Here are but few Hybrid Tea roses, but rather great beds of shrub roses set with the candy-striped Rosa Mundi, and climbing roses grown most originally and effectively on pyramids of trellis work. And the rose beds themselves are not allowed, as still so often happens, to present ugly areas of bare earth between the rose plants, but are planted to overflowing with gay annuals and grey-leaved plants, like the silvery artemisia, to enhance and act as a foil to the roses' summer brilliance.

The Roseraie de l'Hay near Paris is one of the most famous rose gardens in the world, and one to which every student of roses and rosiculture must, at least once in his life, turn his steps; for not only is it a rose garden, but it is a living museum of every rose that grows, documented and catalogued for the instruction of both professional and amateur botanists. The story of the garden started by a chance remark made many years ago to the enormously rich owner of the Bon Marché in Paris, Jules Gravereaux. Somebody said to him, 'If I were as rich as you are, I would give up business and devote my whole life to growing roses.' This sowed a seed in M. Gravereaux's mind, and some years later he gave up his business and planted a rose garden. This is how the Roseraie de l'Hay was originally started, and it is now one of the greatest rose gardens in the world.

But of all rose gardens, the Bagatelle in Paris is one of the most romantic, historically as well as horticulturally, and its story deserves to be told in full.

Bagatelle, as it stands today, was built in 1777 by the Comte d'Artois, brother of Louis XVI. His project, and his method of carrying it out, met with the disapproval of the Austrian Ambassador, Mercy-Argenteau, who wrote the following letter about it to his Empress, Maria Thérésa, mother of Marie Antoinette.

'M. le Comte d'Artois has had the idea of pulling down a little house he has in the Bois de Boulogne, called Bagatelle, and entirely rebuilding it, so that he can give a fête there for the Queen when she returns to Versailles... At first it seemed absurd to try to do this in so short a time, but this is what has been done, by dint of using a thousand workmen, working night and day. What is shocking is that, as there is a shortage of dressed stone, of lime and of plaster, and no time to procure them, M. le Comte ordered the Swiss guards to seize any wagons

93 Rose-hung parasols grown round the 'Kiosk of the Empress' at Bagatelle, from which the Empress Eugénie used to watch her son take riding lessons.

94 In the Rosaleda at Madrid roses grown on pergolas reflect themselves in the pools.

96 In the great rose garden of Madrid, La
Rosaleda, Hybrid Tea roses grow in profusion in
front of a rose-hung pergola.

95 *(opposite)* Roses look especially well grown
on pillars and loosely tied: always successful are
the pink Albertine, glowing crimson *Guinée* and
the golden Elegance.

on the high roads which contained such materials. Payment was
made on the spot, but as the loads in question had all been
bought by private individuals, the high-handedness of the
transaction has shocked everyone.'

The exquisite little building, with its window garlanded with
roses carved in stone, was in fact completed in three months only,
and Marie Antoinette lost her bet of a hundred thousand livres

that such a feat was impossible. The life of Bagatelle and its gardens had begun, and Parisians on their day out hummed this little tune:

Si vous voulez vous promener
Dans ce Bois, charmante Isabelle,
Nous pourrons, sans nous détourner,
Aller jusqu'à Bagatelle

which might be loosely translated:

Why not take a walk today
Through the woods, sweet Isabelle.
You will find it's on the way
To the Park at Bagatelle.

But the gay and careless Comte d'Artois only enjoyed his new toy (for Bagatelle was never intended to be anything but a folly – a place for picnics) for twelve years or so, and soon after the outbreak of the Revolution in 1789 he wisely emigrated. He was not to see Bagatelle for nearly twenty-six years. The Revolution spared Bagatelle, which it decreed should be given over '*aux réjouissances populaires*', and soon it became a popular meeting place, with a restaurant, café, and entertainments such as dancing, peep-shows and balloon ascents. So it continued until well on into the Empire when Napoleon bought it, put it once more in order and used it as a hunting box. It was here – among the roses of Bagatelle – that the repudiated Joséphine, having left her own rose garden at Malmaison, used to come secretly to watch the little King of Rome play in the garden, the longed-for son that her successor had borne the Emperor.

At the fall of the Empire, the Comte d'Artois, older and wiser, returned to France and retook possession of Bagatelle, but made few changes except to remove some of the more daring paintings which had survived from his younger days. Eventually, under the Second Empire, Bagatelle entered into its second great period, when it was acquired by a vastly rich Milord, the Marquis of Hertford, who found Paris a pleasanter place in which to live than Victorian London. He altered the house itself, not always very happily, and developed the garden. Among his innovations was a paddock where the Prince Imperial, son of Napoleon and Eugénie, came to take his daily riding lessons. The Emperor and Empress often came to watch, and would sit in the little kiosk which looked, and still looks, over the paddock. The paddock itself, years later, was to become the famous rose garden of Bagatelle.

Lord Hertford died, and left Bagatelle to his natural son, Sir Richard Wallace (of the Wallace Collection), and his heirs sold it

97 A corner of the Bagatelle gardens, begun in 1777.

98 The Roseraie de l'Hay near Paris is a living museum of nearly every rose.

to the city of Paris, one of whose most valuable possessions it still is. The gardens were replanned by that great French garden planner, J.C.N. Forestier, early in this century. One of his first undertakings was to design and lay out the famous rose garden that exists today.

The rose garden at Bagatelle, unlike the equally celebrated one at La Roseraie de l'Hay, is no museum of roses, but is devoted to growing all known decorative roses, and of them it has as complete a collection as any in the world. In June the garden presents an intoxicating sight with its neat, box-bordered beds brimming with flowers; its festooned pergolas; its parasols of weeping roses, and its beds devoted to the newest floribundas. In all, there are seven thousand rose trees at Bagatelle, and more than three hundred varieties grown. In high summer it presents a joyous picture, with happy Parisians and their children throughly enjoying their afternoon among the flowers. All around are the oaks of the Comte d'Artois, who, as King Charles X, died in exile; and still, on its little rise, stands the kiosk of the Empress Eugénie, an Empress who lost her throne and whose son (the little boy she used to watch riding on his pony at Bagatelle) was killed fighting in the British Army in Zululand in 1879.

VARIETIES AND CULTIVATION

100   A Victorian drawing of a rose grown as a standard.

THE ROSE, IN SPITE OF THE ENCOMIA generously bestowed on it throughout the ages by poets and artists, and in spite of the fact that all that is best and most beautiful has always been compared to it, for many centuries stirred little interest botanically. In the revised edition of La Quintinie's *Herball*, published about 1690, only fourteen types of roses are listed, though there are over four hundred tulips; and sixty years later, Linnaeus (1707–78), the great Swedish botanist, to whom we owe our system of plant nomenclature, only speaks of twenty varieties of rose. Today there are literally several thousands, thanks to the work of the plant collectors and hybridizers in the last hundred and fifty years.

In our own times, the great rose raisers tend to be either German, French or American. England seems to be lagging behind in the production of new roses, though no country has better rose gardens or richer collections of the old and species roses. In Germany the great firm of Kordes, and their friendly rival Tantau, offer wonderful new flowers, and their shrub roses, result of so much hybridization that they are difficult to fit into any of the recognized categories, are great additions to any garden: roses such as the scarlet Berlin, the pink Elmshorn and the orange-buff Grandmaster. Another German rose, and an important one, is the magnificent Hybrid Tea Super Star, considered by experts to be the finest rose since Peace [figure 107].

France, too, is the birthplace of many of the loveliest new roses where the firm of Meilland raised not only the transcendent Hybrid Tea Peace, but many other beauties, such as Madame A. Meilland, which starts life as a bright canary yellow but matures to carmine; Michèle Meilland, and the exquisite Christian Dior, voted the best rose in France in 1958.

But it is in America that the most sensational developments have taken place in rose creation in the last half century. Not so much in the field of the Hybrid Tea, as in France, or of the shrub rose, as in Germany, but in the making of many new wonderful climbing roses. Dorothy Perkins, that rose which is seen in every English suburban garden, is an American-raised rose; it was created in 1901 by the firm of Jackson and Perkins who are, in collaboration with their celebrated hybridizer Boerner, still giving us good new climbing and rambling roses

99   ... the beauty of the rose.

101, 102 *(above)* A rose grown as a half standard, and *(below)* a rose grown as a pot-plant.

today. Goldilocks, introduced in 1952, is one of these roses. The rambler, New Dawn, an exquisite rose, was raised in America in 1930 and inherited its useful late-flowering qualities from its parent (another American) Dr Van Fleet, called after an American politician and keen horticulturalist. Many of the new floribundas, too, were raised in America; some of the best, in fact, since the first polyanthas were raised in Denmark by the firm of Poulsen fifty years ago: the coral Fashion (Boerner 1949), the sparkling Jiminy Cricket (Jackson and Perkins 1954) and Masquerade (Boerner, too) are all American-raised roses. Ever since Charles Dingee opened the first American rose nursery at West Grove, Pennsylvania in 1854, American rose growers have been doing sterling work, and never so much so as in the last fifty years.

With the thousands of roses, old as well as new, it is difficult for the amateur to know with what to start a collection, but any garden of old roses should include some of the Cabbage roses, the Moss, the Centifolias, the Gallicas, the Musks and the Damask. These are the roses which, in England especially, have become so popular, and rightly. For even if their season of flowering is short, their form, character and scent are incomparable; and compared to the hybrid Teas they ask for little looking after and the minimum of pruning.

A connoisseur's list of a few of the most beautiful of these roses would certainly include the Moss rose, *Chapeau de Napoléon*, with crested buds which are exactly like the Emperor's hat; *Francofurtana Agathe*, a rich pink Gallica; The Hybrid Musk Buff Beauty, *Roger Lambelin*, a deep curling crimson-purple with petals piped with white; Hidcote Gold, brought back from Yunnan by the great American gardener Lawrence Johnston; the deep purple Cardinal Richelieu, a Gallica; the lovely pink and white striped *Camaieux*; *Rosa moyesii* and *Rosa hugonis* for their brilliant and 'different' colours, scarlet and gold respectively. A favourite old rose of the poet and gardener V. Sackville-West, was *Rosa alba*, otherwise often known as 'Great Maiden's Blush'. This is an enchanting rose, shell-pink and many petalled; it has other names, too, (their names contribute greatly to the charm of old roses), and is known as *La Séduisante* and *Cuisse de Nymphe*, Nymph's Thigh. 'When she blushed a particularly deep pink,' wrote Miss Sackville-West, 'she was called *Cuisse de Nymphe Émue*. I will not insult the French language by attempting to translate this highly expressive name – but I would suggest only that Cyrano de Bergerac would have appreciated the implication . . .'

Miss Sackville-West did much to restore the old roses to favour, as did the late Nancy Lindsay, daughter of Norah Lindsay, a well-known amateur gardener who laid out many of the best of the smaller gardens in England before the war. This is how Miss

103, 104 Roses were an important feature in nineteenth-century fashions: *(above left)* on the hat, shoulder and parasol of a seaside ensemble in 1890; and *(above centre)* in the hair, corsage and train of an evening dress in the '80s.

105 *(above right)* Roses were just as popular with the early Victorians: a garden party frock with leg-of-mutton sleeves in 1834.

Lindsay described three of her favourite old roses:

Kazanlik: 'The Turkish attar-of-roses rose, sent from Constantinople over forty years ago to my beautiful young mother, has cascades of ambrosial, pellucid rose-pink flowers with lambent coral hearts, over jungles of mint-green.'

Madame Ernst Calvat: 'An August bush with young shoots sparkling rose and violet, and vintage leaves of silver, lustred peacock-green, illuminated carmine. The sumptuous, perfumed cabbages are Tyrian rose mellowing to seraphic mauve.'

Xanthina: 'First observed in a double form in a Cathayan garden about 1800, it resembles that now in cultivation known as Slingeri. The truly wild form, named *Spontanea,* emerged at Paul's Cheshunt Nursery in 1915. The tally of China's great golden rose is not yet told. *Spontanea* itself is a gorgeous great shrub with fee-fo-fum triangular thorns close-set on cinnamon boughs and ferny leaves of jade-green hue. Its showers of dog-roses are of a lovely golden-lemon, and the orbicular hips glow like rubies.'

Thus, triumphantly, Miss Nancy Lindsay. Her enthusiasm for old roses communicates itself, as we read her glowing imaginative descriptions. There are nurseries that specialize in old roses, for more and more old roses enrich the gardens of connoisseurs each year. Our gratitude is due to the nurserymen who raise them and to enthusiasts like the two ladies I have quoted for their championship of these lovely plants. But for their enthusiasm, many of the old roses must have been lost for ever.

Every year roses are being improved, and if you were to compare a catalogue of seventy years ago with one of today, you

106 Prima Ballerina is a beautiful Hybrid Tea rose, raised in Germany by Tantau in 1957.

would find very few roses that figure in both. The reason for this is obvious, in spite of what the grumblers say: modern roses *are* better, more healthy and stronger growing than their counterparts of seventy years ago, thanks to the hard work and inspiration of hybridists, who for the last hundred-and-fifty years, have been working hard to produce more perfect roses. 'But,' says the old rose addict, 'modern roses have no scent.' This, of course, is not true, at least, not entirely true. New roses – many of them –

are deliciously scented, but even if they are not, their vigour, length of flowering period and wonderful colouring amply make up for their lack of fragrance. If it was desired to form a collection of new roses these are some it would be well to choose, with the years of their introduction.

HYBRID TEAS

Charles Mallerin (1949) is such a dark crimson as to be almost black, with well-shaped flowers which are strongly scented.

Chrysler Imperial (1952) has velvety crimson flowers on stiff, upright stems and strongly scented; with glossy, healthy foliage.

Ena Harkness (1946) is one of the strongest growing scarlet roses,

107 Judged by international experts to be the finest new Hybrid Tea rose since Peace, Super Star was raised in Germany by the brilliant rose breeder Tantau.

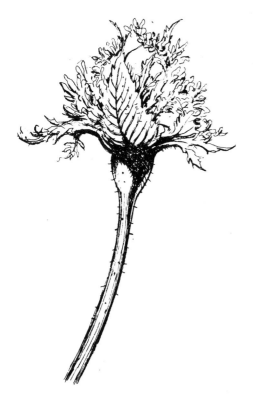

The Moss rose, *Chapeau de Napoleon*, has crested buds recalling the Emperor's hat.

109 In the last fifty years miniature roses have gained greatly in popularity.

with a very long flowering period – well into the autumn.

Grandmère Jenny (1950), the improved child of Peace, but with better shaped, better coloured flowers and strong healthy leaves.

Lady Zia (1959), a cross between Peace and the too-bright Independence, with rosy flame flowers, which become more brilliant as they age.

Lilac Time (1955) for its subtle colouring and exquisite shape.

Lydia (1950) for its rich unfading gold and profusion of flowers.

Christian Dior (1958) for its rich red colouring and robust growth, and in spite of its undeniable lack of scent.

McGredy's Yellow (1933) for its superb flowers of soft lemon-yellow, and for the exquisite way its shining green leaves, edged with russet, contrast with its blooms.

Virgo (1949) for its paper-white flowers that are perfectly shaped and strong enough to stand up to the weather all summer through.

Super Star (1959) for its brilliance and vigour.

Some other rewarding Hybrid Tea roses which have appeared to grace the garden in recent years are Soraya, called after the beautiful woman who was once Queen of Persia, home of so many roses, a brilliant red rose which lends itself well to cutting; the clear pink Rendezvous, and the full elegant Eden Rose which is a clear carmine.

FLORIBUNDAS

These roses, having graduated from the period when they seemed good only for municipal gardens, have entirely shed their slightly common character and now make as important a group of garden plants as any. Long flowering – from May until the first frosts – healthy, vigorous, and in an astonishingly wide range of new and fascinating colours, floribunda roses look well planted in formal beds or among shrubs or in a mixed border. Many of the best new ones were raised in America. These are some of the best:

Alain. A splendid red, and slightly scented.

Buisman's Triumph. Carmine, and semi-double, with the dark leaves of Rosemary Rose.

Columbine. Pale yellow edged with pink, with flowers in clusters.

Fashion. Bright salmon pink and slightly scented.

Geranium. Large, flat flowers with crinkled petals in dark red colouring, and a compact growth and pleasing scent.

Goldilocks. Lemon yellow flowers and masses of them.

Iceberg. The buds are flushed with shell-pink, but its flowers open to an icy whiteness shaded with green, with curving petals.

Lavender Pinocchio. A wonderfully strange lavender grey colour, slightly scented and typical of the 'new' colouring in roses.

Masquerade. Changes its colours in the oddest way from yellow,

110 Three modern Hybrid Tea roses.

through salmon pink to scarlet and flame.

Rosemary Rose. A brilliant rose of unfading red, which has deservedly become very popular. Its leaves, scarcely less attractive than its flowers, are coppery red. *Queen Elizabeth.* Opinions vary violently about this rose – some saying that it is perfection, others that it grows too tall; but no-one can deny that its flowers are beautiful: deep pink, well shaped and as fine as those of a Hybrid Tea.

CLIMBING ROSES

These do not seem to have been as much developed lately as the other varieties of roses have been, though there are some very beautiful ones which, for one reason or another, are not often planted, such as the climbing form of

Ena Harkness (1954). Glowing crimson and strongly scented.

Guinée (1937). Velvet red, dark foliage.

Madame Grégoire Staechelin (1927). A transcendent rose, which is pink splashed with carmine, and richly scented.

Paul's Lemon Pillar (1915). White shaded with green, and a lovely sight in June, when alas, it has its only flowering period.

Mermaid. Introduced the year the first World War ended, and still one of the loveliest of all roses for a wall – with its saucer-sized golden flowers and five-months' flowering period.

MINIATURE ROSES

Recently, in the last fifty years or so, miniature roses have won many hearts and rightly so, as they are enchanting plants. Originally raised by Dr Roulet who, by chance, came across a plant in Switzerland and propagated from it, miniature roses can be grown among rock work, in window boxes or used in miniature rose gardens to charming effect. But, like all highly

87

hybridized plants, most are scentless. A few of the best to choose are the original and still smallest of all, *R. rouletii* (pink), the red Peon, and the delicate white Cinderella with its bright, ferny light-green foliage.

CULTIVATION

To grow roses well and to get the best from them it is essential to study their primary needs as to soil and situation, and to plant them carefully so that they have at least a good start in life. Plant a rose carelessly in ill-prepared ground and, such good-tempered plants are they, it is quite possible that they will survive; but plant them well, in well-prepared and suitably enriched soil, and they are certain to flourish for years and years. Roses prefer a rich loam with some clay, though this is not, as many people strongly hold, essential. Very heavy soil can be made more acceptable by having well-rotted manure or humus dug well into it; and light, thin soils can be improved by adding humus again, rotted-down turf, compost or peat to retain moisture.

When planning to plant roses, the ground should be well dug over a month or so before planting time and the compost or well-rotted manure dug in well below where the roots will go. Only plant newly-arrived rose bushes when the weather is suitable, and when the soil is in good condition. It is not fair to plant roses when the earth is waterlogged or frozen hard, and if it is in this condition the new plants should be 'heeled in' in a trench, with a light covering of soil and as close together as you like, and trodden down firmly. Safely bestowed in this manner they can quite well remain unplanted for some weeks, until the weather makes the ground easy to work once more.

When roses are planted it is essential to see that the hole intended for the roots is quite large enough: the roots should be able to spread out flat, in a natural way, and certainly not be bunched up or bundled together in a knot. When in position, put some dry soil, sieved fine, among the roots and 'dance' the bush up and down to work the soil all round the roots: follow the fine earth with heavier mould until the hole is quite full, and tread it down firm. When planting is finished the level of the soil should just come above the top of the rootstock. In planting standard roses it is best to give the tree a stake before covering the roots with earth, to avoid hurting them. Planting can be carried on after October all through the winter, in suitable weather.

Pruning should be carried out in March, or earlier if the season is advanced and the new young growth is much in evidence. As a rule roses flower three or so months after pruning. Hybrid Tea roses and Floribundas should be pruned back to two or three buds and it is important that the top bud – the bud

111 Climbing roses have not been so much developed recently as many other varieties.

112 Cocktail is a typical modern rose; strong, disease-resistant, it can be grown as a floribunda, given its head and allowed to climb, or if suitably pruned, will make a self-supporting hedge.

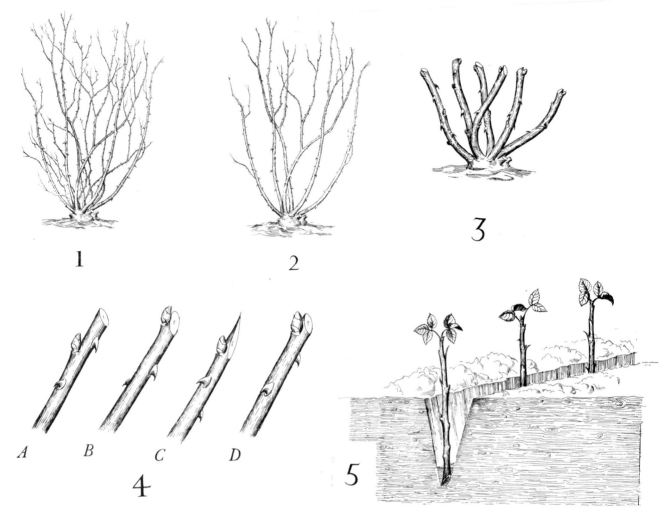

113 The art of pruning: 1. A rose-bush before pruning, with tangled branches and much weak growth. 2. The bush has been thinned out by removing the weak growth. 3. A Hybrid Tea pruned to within six inches of the ground; the buds have been carefully left pointing outwards, to make a shapely bush. 4. The wrong ways (A, B and C) and the right way (D) of pruning. 5. Rose-cuttings rooted in a trench, with silver-sand at the bottom.

nearest the cut – should be left pointing outwards from the bush. This ensures a shapely plant later, with all its shoots pointing outwards from the centre. Rambler roses may be cut back at the same time of year to half the length of their shoots, while climbers and shrub roses only need a light pruning, and having their old dead wood cut out. It is a good rule to remember that if roses are planted late (and it is possible to plant them until March) they must be pruned hard back at planting time.

There are many ways of growing roses, as well as in the formal beds and conventional rose gardens which were the fashion seventy years ago, and some of which still survive today. All the old roses can be grown as shrubs, planted in groups of three or five, or singly, and interplanted with grey foliage plants, lilies, or herbaceous plants. They look well mixed with other shrubs, especially those of coloured leaves like the rhus and the scarlet-leaved berberis, or in a mixed border with herbaceous plants such as delphiniums, lilies and peonies, and planted like this they bring solidity and form to a border even in winter, when a conventional herbaceous border can look ugly.

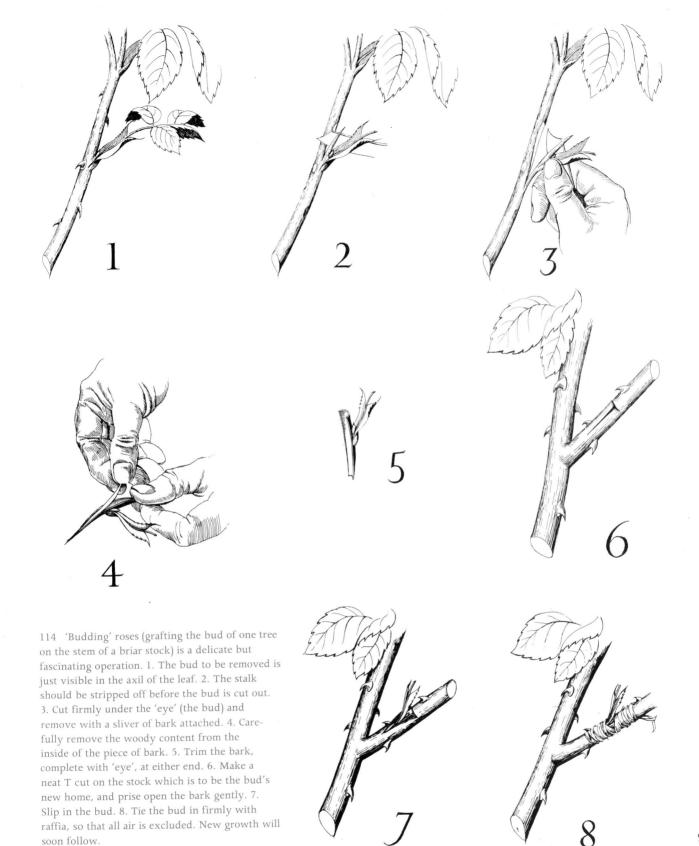

114 'Budding' roses (grafting the bud of one tree on the stem of a briar stock) is a delicate but fascinating operation. 1. The bud to be removed is just visible in the axil of the leaf. 2. The stalk should be stripped off before the bud is cut out. 3. Cut firmly under the 'eye' (the bud) and remove with a sliver of bark attached. 4. Carefully remove the woody content from the inside of the piece of bark. 5. Trim the bark, complete with 'eye', at either end. 6. Make a neat T cut on the stock which is to be the bud's new home, and prise open the bark gently. 7. Slip in the bud. 8. Tie the bud in firmly with raffia, so that all air is excluded. New growth will soon follow.

115 Caroline Testout, one of the oldest of
'modern' roses, with flowers of rosy satin, blooms
92 from early June until the first frosts.

Roses grown on walls can look beautiful, but in planting it should be borne in mind to plant them at least eighteen inches from the base of the wall, with plenty of rich soil and fertilizer worked in, for there the soil is always poor and dry. As many roses are apt to ramp away, leaving bare stems, these should be camouflaged with lower, bushy shrubs planted in front. Some roses ask nothing better than to be planted at the base of trees and allowed to clamber through the branches towards the sky. Some are especially good at this, like *Rosa filipes*, which sends its green shoots and snowy trusses of white flowers up for a

116 Roses grow well on screens or tall fences, their flowers blooming at eye level or above. Here Lady Sylvia shows pink flowers against a blue sky.

93

distance of twenty or thirty feet, and will burst like fireworks from the top of quite tall trees. The same can be said for the Himalayan rose *R. moschata floribunda*, which spreads its scent for yards around, and Seagull, a relation of *R. filipes* and as generous a flowerer. For pillars, there are many elegant roses like the scarlet Soldier Boy; the delicate, long-flowering New Dawn, with its shell-pink flowers flowering just after the ordinary run of roses, and Lady Waterlow, flesh-pink and edged with carmine.

Envoi

De mémoire de roses on n'a point vu mourir le jardinier is a quotation I remember reading many years ago, in one of the fourteen volumes of that writer of nostalgic Victorian memoirs, Augustus Hare. I have never been able to trace it since, and I am sorry, as it seems to me to be most expressive : seems, because I have never been able satisfactorily to translate it; it puzzles even the most erudite French scholar. I would like to think it means literally, 'Within the rose's memory, the gardener never dies.' 'The short-lived rose', in fact, 'forgets that gardeners die too.' The rose ephemeral, once more. But is it true? A single rose, certainly – but roses, surely not.

We have seen something of the lasting, immortal qualities of roses, and how they have recurred as a theme and inspiration through history, music, literature and so many of the pleasures of man's spirit. Perhaps something of this has become part of our consciousness; and when we see a red rose, 'angry and brave', we will recall the clangour of the Wars of the Roses, and the courage and folly of war; and when we see a white rose we may remember the valour of Minden, and give a sigh, not only for the Stuarts, but for all those who have lost their countries and are in exile. And when we notice the oddity of a plant's forma-tion, like the sepals of a Moss Rose, perhaps we will appreciate the wonder and endless interest of flowers, and it will awake an interest in gardening in us we have never had before; for, as Bacon said, 'it is the purest of human pleasures'. Perhaps, too, one day, when we are told that a plant comes from China, we will have a thought for Father Scallon, and for the other great plantsmen of the past, who spent their lives discovering new plants for our gardens.

Nearer home, a wild rose flowering in a hedgerow may bring poor Eglantine to mind, and her literary pretensions; and the lacquered hips of autumn, painted so beautifully by Alfred Parsons, may remind us that there are other rose artists besides Redouté.

And when you next enter a rose garden, although you may not exclaim, with the eloquence of Sadi: 'I meant to fill my lap

117 *Rose Raubritter*, a hybrid of *Rosa macrantha*, shows its globular flowers with petals like clustered shells, photographed by Cecil Beaton.

118 *Memento Mori* by Jean van Kessel (1678–1741).

119 The rose's soul asleep, by Rex Whistler.

with roses, to bring as presents to my companions – but the fragrance so intoxicated me that the skirt of my robe slipped from my hands'; perhaps you will recall something you have read of Bagatelle or the Rose Garden at Hartford, and you may resolve to see more of the beauty around you, and visit a great rose garden next June.

No one country has the prerogative of beautiful roses; all countries have contributed to their present perfection; if you are English, do not forget that Dorothy Perkins, that most English-seeming of roses, was raised in America; and if you are French, that the gardener at Malmaison came from Scotland; if American, acknowledge gratefully the fact that the blood that runs in the veins of your splendid new climbing roses came originally from Europe.

We love the rose because it is one of the finest of God's creations, and we love the roses of today because, without presumption, we ourselves have had a hand in their making. But in spite of the symbolism, the romance, the associations, what, after all, is a rose? A flower, 'whose simple doom is to be beautiful'.

95